Rory Patrick Allen was born to Irish parents in U.K. He holds dual nationality, Irish and British. He has travelled and worked extensively throughout the Arab world and continues to do so. He is the author of several short stories, and one stage play. This is his first full length work.

OMAN
UNDER ARABIAN SKIES

RORY PATRICK ALLEN

OMAN
UNDER ARABIAN SKIES

AN ARABIAN ODYSSEY

Vanguard Press

VANGUARD PAPERBACK

A CIP catalogue record for this title is
available from the British Library.

ISBN 978 1843866084

*Vanguard Press is an imprint of
Pegasus Elliot MacKenzie Publishers Ltd.*
www.pegasuspublishers.com

First Published in 2010

**Vanguard Press
Sheraton House Castle Park
Cambridge England**

Printed & Bound in Great Britain

This book is dedicated to;

Jane Teresa Allen (Nee Valentine), Irvinestown, County Fermanagh, N. Ireland

George Allen, New Ross, County Wexford, The Republic of Ireland.

May Valentine, Irvinestown, County Fermanagh, N. Ireland.

Margaret Mary Allen (Nee O'Kane), Ballerin, County Derry, N. Ireland.

Roisin Clare Marie Allen, Bournemouth, Dorset, England.

Almohanned Ali Al-Farsi, Saham, The Sultanate Of Oman.

"I am all that they made me, and now, all that I ever want to be."   Rory Patrick Allen

ACKNOWLEDGEMENTS

I shall always be grateful to Eamonn and Carolyn Allen who encouraged me to put pen to paper and tell my story about this exotic land. They supported me when my enthusiasm was flagging and urged me on to the finish. Indeed they spent many hours editing, proof reading and offering invaluable and insightful advice. My thanks to Ciaran Allen for his unwavering loyalty through thick and thin and his literary contribution to my manuscript. My special thanks to the people of Oman whose generosity and hospitality remain, in my experience, unsurpassed. This book is also a special tribute to the Sultan of Oman, His Majesty Sultan Qaboos, who having resisted the onslaught of Western materialism and Cola culture has preserved the customs and traditions that make Oman and her people unique.

And so I flew across the earth as a lone eagle and surveyed all that was beneath me. I saw people living in cities with their souls decaying; I then saw green valleys, tall mountains, wide open deserts, distant horizons, glorious sunsets and sunrises and so it was here that I decided to build my nest.

RORY PATRICK ALLEN

CONTENTS

THE SULTANATE OF OMAN

Oman is the land of The Queen of Sheba, a country of deserts, rolling sands and shifting dunes, mountain ranges, oases, wadis, valleys and the warm waters of the Indian Ocean. A country where ancient caravans began their journeys with exotic cargoes of frankincense and myrrh, finely woven fabrics and silks, and spices. Their destinations feature like a catalogue of the Classical Age: Babylon, Greece, Jerusalem, Carthage, Damascus and many more. There was neither a temple nor a palace in the ancient world where the sweet fragrance of frankincense would not assail your senses and this precious resin was worth its weight in gold. Picturesque villages are to be found nestled in the mountains where the people carry on their lives and traditions without incumbency from the roar and stress of the twentieth century. Their fertile land, irrigated by underground water supplies, supports a rich variety of produce including grapes, pomegranates, oranges and many other fruits and crops. The inhabitants are warm and welcoming and are renowned for their hospitality to strangers and visitors alike.

The Sultanate of Oman is one of the only two Sultanates that remain in the world today, the other being The Sultanate of Brunei. Oman lies in the south-eastern corner of the Arabian Peninsula. It covers the same area as Britain yet carries a population of only three million. The coastline extends one thousand seven hundred kilometres from the Straits of Hormuz in the north to the borders of Yemen in the south. The temperatures from May to September reach 45 degrees Celsius and during winter they can average 25 degrees.

The Sultanate of Oman is divided into eight different regions. Every region has its own distinctive flavour and essence.

Muscat is the capital of Oman where the majority of the population increasingly dwells. This is the area of business and commerce. Batinah, just north of Muscat, extends along the coast up to the border with the UAE. This is the most fertile area of Oman. The capital of Batinah would be Sohar or Rustaq. West, across the mountain range, is Dara, its capital Ibri; this is a sparsely populated and much untravelled part of Oman, its indigenous people being Bedouin, and the desert is of a gravelly texture. Dakhliyah is in the interior of Oman, the capital of which is Nizwa. This is the most conservative area of Oman and the people are largely involved in agriculture and the raising of livestock. The Sharqiyah, the capital of which is Sur, is also an area where Bedouin live, yet unlike Dara its sand is soft and many magnificent dunes are visible; it features like a clip from the film *Lawrence of Arabia.* Dhofar, to the west of which lies the Rub al Khali, the Empty Quarter, is situated a thousand kilometres from Muscat, eight hundred of those kilometres being virgin desert. The capital of Dhofar is Salalah. Dhofar has a border with the Yemen and is very close to the horn of Africa. In the mountains of Dhofar live a people, largely pastoral farmers, whose language is not Arabic but an ancient language known as Shahri. This is an oral language and has no written form. This land is said to be the land of the Old Testament. Indeed the tomb of the prophet Job is to be found in these mountains. Dhofar turns from brown to an emerald green overnight when she catches the tip of the Monsoon in August and visitors from all over the Gulf flock to the lush greenery that is to be found there during this time. Al Wusta has the second largest land area among Oman's eight regions and the smallest number of inhabitants: seventeen thousand as compared with the five hundred and fifty thousand population of Batinah. A large part of this area is desert and gravel plains. It really has no capital area that I know of; perhaps Mahout with a population of nearly eight thousand could be called its capital town. This area is south of the Sharqiyah and stretches south down to Dhofar. Its northern border runs from Mahout to Saudi Arabia, its Western border, and to the east, The Arabian Sea. There are wide open bays of white and golden sands with inlets and rocky coves. In this area live the wild Arabian Oryx and flamingos, dolphins, sea turtles and whales are all a common sight.

Musandam, the eighth region of Oman, is the most northerly of all regions; its capital is Khasab, and it is in fact a peninsula separated from the rest of Oman by a seventy-kilometre stretch of the United Arab Emirates. It is a mountainous area with a sturdy people whose traditional weapon is a small axe which marks the difference between the people of Musandam and the rest of Oman. This peninsula sits on the Straits of Hormuz.

Oman is the only Gulf state to have had an empire. This Empire stretched from the coasts of what is now Somaliland to Mozambique and Zanzibar was Oman's second capital. It included the United Arab Emirates and Baluchistan (which is now part of Pakistan). Oman traded her wares all over East Africa and brought her culture and traditions with her. She also brought Islam to the east coast of Africa so the teachings of the Prophet Mohammed were brought here borne on the sails of the Arabian dhow. The traders used the Monsoon winds to travel to their destinations and to return from them. Sinbad is believed to have been born here in Oman, in a town called Sohar, two hundred and thirty kilometres north of Muscat. Indeed in Muscat you will find the boat built in the traditional way by Tim Severin and used by him in a tale he relates in the *Sinbad Voyage*.

Bronze Age works and settlements have been found in the interior, which archaeologists say testify to a viable society with trading links to the ancient world more than five thousand years ago.

IN THE BEGINNING

"So you are going to write about your life in Oman," said Fahad, a striking-looking Bedu from one of the desert areas of Oman called The Wahiba Sands. I had known Fahad for ten years. We were in my apartment looking out on to the Indian Ocean, a glorious still blue sea, shimmering in the midday sun, the temperature over 40 degrees; small motorized fishing boats gliding past leaving in their wake a white foaming trail underneath a cloudless sky. The stark sun reflected off the white walls of the villas of Muscat, the capital of the Sultanate of Oman. Byelaws dictate that all villas must be white or a shade thereof in keeping with the Arab architecture.

"I am," I said. "I feel that maybe it is time to move on and I really want to write down all my memories so when I am old I can recollect them. If not all those special moments will be lost."

"Well just don't forget my name."

"Of course I will not, you are the main character." At that he beamed a wonderful smile which accentuated the laughter lines around his eyes and revealed perfect teeth. The Omani is forever smiling and laughing; I have yet to see one grimace. They so enjoy life and are so thankful to God for giving them health and the ability to enjoy life today, for tomorrow who knows what the hand of fate will deal them.

Fahad got up to leave. He was in full traditional dress, Bedu usually are, and they are so proud and dignified and stand as straight as an arrow. He was wearing a long white robe, called a dishdasha, with a turban of many colours on his head and open-toe sandals. Around his waist he wore a leather belt inlaid with fine silver. At the front of the belt a silver sheath was attached which held a curved silver dagger, the handle of which was made of ivory. In his right hand he carried a thin cane stick with a hook-like handle. These sticks are largely ceremonial now, however not completely as they can be useful if, when sleeping in the desert, one encountered a snake or a scorpion.

"Where are you going Fahad?"

"Back to my village of course," he answered. Omanis have a great love for and extremely strong ties to their village. For every Omani his village is the most beautiful in Oman. This is where his life is; his family is and has been for generations. At every opportunity an Omani will return to his village, if only for a few hours. When the inhabitants of a village see their native son return they will gather in the square shouting "Welcome home", and asking him what news he has from the world outside. The village chat will be Juma Ali; Abu Moussa has returned today and told us about the latest news from Muscat. A man in the Arab world will be known by his first name and the name of his father. Hence Juma, son of Ali, as there will undoubtedly be many Jumas in the village and the need to identify which

Juma you are talking about is obvious. Alternatively he will be known as Abu Moussa (father of Moussa), if he has a son called Moussa. Many Westerners get confused when listening to the news and hearing at one time an individual being referred to as Abu (father of), then another time that same individual being called a different name.

When you enter an Omani village you will come across many houses made of mud and brick, crumbling and derelict, yet the children of the families that once occupied these dwellings will build their new houses with the new walls attached to the outer wall of the crumbling derelicts. This may sound a bit bizarre but the symbolism is clear: it provides for great continuity with the past and the traditions of family and culture associated therein. This gives the Omani a strong sense of identity as to who and what he is and where he comes from and it is because of this that individual Omanis have a great deal of security, a oneness with their community and society. In each village in Oman there is a collective unconsciousness that binds the people together. Carl Jung was very impressed by how much people in Africa were in touch with it and how much they realized that the meaning of their lives depended on not losing touch with this collective unconscious. It is from this collective unconscious, he believes, that all our great energies come as do all the patterns that give life meaning. This is what I found so vital and alive in the Omani. Jung believed that the West was losing sight of this collective unconscious and society was drifting away from it, causing alienation from the collective whole, leading to disastrous consequences for the individual living in that society.

It is thanks to the present-day Sultan that Oman has resisted the onslaught of Western cultural imperialism and fiercely maintained Omani customs, traditions and way of life that have given the Omani such individual and collective strength, pride and dignity.

When Fahad had gone I looked out towards the sea and turned my mind back to that day fifteen years ago when I left England and started a journey that was to be the most profound that I had ever undertaken.

THE JOURNEY

It is a Thursday morning in the month of November and the year is 1991. At 4a.m., my alarm clock sounds; I turn over and luxuriate in the warmth of my bed. "Just another five minutes," I say to myself. Five turns into ten and I know that if I am going to get the 5.30a.m. bus from Bournemouth to Heathrow then I must get up now. I throw off my duvet and feel the cold of the early winter morning air. I look out of the window that is misted up and I make out the rain slicing through the icy heavens. I wash my face quickly and brush my teeth; it is far too cold to even contemplate a shower. While drinking endless cups of tea I check my passport and ticket are in place. The door bell rings and the taxi driver takes my bags down to his car. I slide into the back seat. It is far too early for me to make conversation nonetheless the taxi driver manages.

"Going anywhere nice?" he asks. I grunt in reply and he gets the message. At 5.15 I arrive at the bus station and have to wait fifteen more minutes in the early morning cold before I am to embark on the bus, which will be for me the beginning of a journey from which I shall return as a completely changed person.

As the bus heads off for Heathrow our journey takes us through the New Forest just as the sun is beginning to rise and a glorious pink sky heralds a new dawn. It is a wonderful sight to see the early morning sun gradually light the mist on the gorse bushes that abound the forest and the wild ponies arising from their slumber. The sun climbs and with it the whole vista of the Forest is revealed in its full magnificence. As we pass signs for the "The Rufus Stone" and Winchester I am reminded of the great wealth of English history that unravelled itself inside and on the fringes of this, one of England's most beautiful forests. The thought dawns on me as to why I am leaving this beautiful place to go the deserts of the Middle East but I have heard that the Sultanate of Oman is a special place and this thought comforts me as I drift into sleep until it is announced that we have arrived at Heathrow, Terminal Four.

The call came for the departure of the flight to Oman, this was the point of no return, and I hesitated but then proceeded to the departure gate, just in time as it happens. I handed my boarding pass to the stewardess; I was shown to my window seat, strapped into my seat belt, leant my head against the window and blissfully slipped into unconsciousness.

I awoke seven hours later after a bump that signalled we had landed in Abu Dhabi. Outside it was dark, the time zone being four hours ahead of the UK. The majority of passengers disembarked into this fabulously oil rich emirate/sheikdom. We took off for Muscat at 9p.m. local time and it was a forty minute flight. As the plane made its final approach to Seeb Airport felt I a sudden surge of adrenalin for I was about to enter the Land of the Sultans.

ARRIVAL

The immigration desks were wonderful. The men all in white gowns and turbans. It was like a scene from the Arabian nights. I walked up to the desk and handed over my passport. The Immigration official checked and returned it with a glorious smile saying, "Welcome to Oman."

In the greetings hall I was met by a corporal in uniform. He took me to the Officers' Mess where I received the key to my room and fell into a deep sleep dreaming of Aladdin, the forty thieves, magic carpets and caves full of precious stones.

At 5.40a.m. I was awoken by the sound of the Muezzin and the call to prayer. I stood on the balcony of my room and watched the sun rise like a great golden globe over the Hajar Mountains that hug the coast of Muscat. The exhilaration I felt is impossible to describe in words. At 6.30 my corporal arrived to take me to the many places where I was to complete what is known as a joining-in process, finger printing and ID card at the police station, opening a bank account, meeting all my bosses and drinking never ending cups of Omani coffee and eating dates. It is a rigid Omani custom that every office/house you go to you must partake of this very strong coffee and eat the wonderful dates, of which there are a variety of two hundred in Oman. During the course of the day I must have visited about ten different offices and I believed that my blood had been turned into pure caffeine.

Omanis range in colours from black to white with all shades in between. In one administration office there were six employees in uniform busying away and I noticed that five of them had very large holes, as if they had been drilled, in a part of their ear, not the lobe but just above it. When I asked them the reason for this I was told that at birth this had been done to let the evil spirits/jinn pass through their bodies otherwise it would be trapped inside their bodies and they would get sick. These jinn are spirits of a parallel world and are divided equally into good and bad jinn. The jinn can also take the form of any animal they so desire and the Omani, if he saw an animal be it donkey, cat or dog, somewhere out of context, he would believe this animal to be a jinn. They are mentioned in The Koran and humans are told to respect them so if a bucket of dirty water, for example, is thrown out of the window the thrower must say a prayer amounting to an apology to or forgiveness if the water lands on the jinn. Indeed, when talking to older generations of Omanis they tell many tales of old beliefs and superstitions that at one time were prevalent in Oman. What we call dust devils the older Omani believes are colonies of jinn travelling from one destination to another.

Bahla, where there is magnificent pre-Islamic fort that is a World Heritage monument, is famous or infamous for its sorcerers known as sahers. These older men would sit under a particular tree in the village of Bahla and eye up potential victims that they would either want to eat or turn into zombies to work their plantations. These saher were said to fly at night on the backs of hyena and the only defence against these wizards was to drink mercury or to have alcohol in your system. In all stories of ancient alchemy, mercury plays a large part. Indeed the further one goes into Omani society the more one realizes it was a land governed by the rules of the ancients, myths and legends, magicians and wizards, curses and phantoms, a land of animists, pantheists, sacred mountains, potent herbal remedies etc.

The story was also that there was a rather grisly initiation ceremony if you wanted to join the ranks of the sorcerers. It was this: you were to choose your favourite child and bring her/him to a cave where the sorcerers gather, rather like a witch's coven, and then to kill the child and all were to feast on it. The younger the child, the more tender the meat or so I am told. These Zombies, or the living dead, were firmly believed in by the Omani who you would hear tales from about people who have died in their village in one region, only to be seen working in a plantation in another village in a different region in Oman. These tales were wonderful snapshots of times gone by and yet there is still a residue of these beliefs to be found lingering in some nether parts of the Omani psyche.

One of the chaps in the office did not have this hole in his ear, a black chap, and his English appeared to be better than the others. After having chatted with him for about five minutes, I remarked on the quality of his English and asked him where he had learnt it. "In London," he said. "I am English and working here on a two year contract."

"Whoops, sorry about that," I said. However he took it in good spirit and made me feel better by telling me that I was not the first one to have made that mistake.

It was by now 11.30a.m. I had an appointment with a British colonel who was to tell me where I was to be posted. "Come in, old chap, how are you finding it all?" This was a rhetorical question and he was definitely not expecting nor desiring a reply. Looking at my papers he said, "Ah, I see you have worked with the Saudi Navy before, yes that is good we need someone on the naval base – you can go up there."

"Where would that be, sir," I asked.

"Oh, do not worry about that, just have your bags packed and you will be driven up tomorrow at 7a.m. sharp."

It was now pretty warm at 12.30p.m. One last job to do. Colonel Jassim said a driving test. "But I have an English driving licence and I thought I could just change it to an Omani licence."

"That is a civilian licence," he said. "You need to take a military licence."

"I have only come here to teach English," I said, "not to drive an armoured vehicle for the UN in some war torn country in Africa." We drove to an army camp that was essentially rough desert. Army camouflaged lorries were parked around an open space of ground like some wagon train. There was a narrow gap that we were to drive through. We arrived upon an old English Land Rover with an Omani in camouflage who looked even older than the Land Rover.

"Right, get in," Jassim said. Having never driven anything larger than a VW, it was all a new experience and I started the engine. Before I engaged into first gear I noticed stirrings from under the parked lorries, only to make out soldiers, who had been sleeping in the shade of these lorries, also dressed in green camouflage and wearing turbans. I had woken them up and I sensed that they thought there may be a bit of sport to be had in watching this spectacle of a *Nazarene* (literally one who follows the teachings of Jesus of Nazareth) trying to drive this museum piece. So there I was the centre of the show. Every time I crunched a gear or got stuck in the sand whoops of joy and laughter rang out among the troops. At least they were enjoying it; I was not, covered in sweat and feeling humiliated. When I had at last finished my test I received a round of applause from the troops whereon they slid back under their lorries like snails retreating back into their shells. The next part of the driving test was even more bizarre. I should have mentioned the examiner spoke not a word of English and after my driving test he proceeded to show me cards depicting road signs. I of course answered in English. Getting tired of this rather futile exercise I was happy when it was all over. As we drove away I said to Jassim, "Well that was a waste of time."

"Not really," he said, "...you passed."

ARABIA

7a.m. sharp I was waiting outside for Jassim to drive me to the Naval Base, my life packed into two bags. 7.15. Where was Jassim? 7.30. Jassim in his military pick up turns the corner, big smiles. "Salaam Alaekum," he says, peace be upon you, "Alaekum Salaam," I reply, and upon you too. This is a standard greeting and in the Arab world if one does not initiate or reply to this greeting great offence is taken. The Omanis' greetings are governed by strict codes of protocol and it can go on for what can seem like an eternity asking after family, relations etc, but for the Westerner Salaam Alaekum and its response is good enough. I throw my bags into the back of the pickup and slide into the bench seat.

"How long will it take to drive there," I ask.

"One and a half hours, Inshallah," he replies.

"Inshallah" like "Salaam Alaekum", is frequently used, in fact virtually at the end of every sentence; it means God willing, so when you make an arrangement to see someone or do a job or anything at all one finishes the sentence with the word Inshallah. It says a lot about the people; they are very fatalistic and whatever is meant to be is meant to be. "It is written in the sand", everything is in the hands of God; if he so desires it will happen; when your time is up and God wants you then you will go. I remember when a colleague of mine was killed in a car accident and I was upset, an Omani friend by the name of Abdullah said, "Why are you so upset? When it is time it is time, not a minute later or a minute earlier; it is the will of God." The Muslim subjugates his whole life to the will of God. In many ways this is a healthy outlook for no one can cheat death and the Arab accepts that and then after an appropriate amount of time for grieving they continue with their lives; not to do so is an offence against God, a sin.

The Bedu is washed after death, wrapped in a shroud and put in the sand; there is no marker. In the Omani villages that are not in the desert a piece of land is set aside, again the body washed, wrapped in a shroud and put into the ground. A stone or piece of rock will mark the spot, but no inscription or dutiful visits on anniversaries. The body was a carrier for the soul and the essence of that person has now gone to Paradise.

So Jassim and I begin our journey where he is to deliver me like a parcel to Wudam Naval Base and then return to Muscat. The road is a new highway in excellent condition with many roundabouts en route. There is something almost akin to a cult of roundabout beautification in Oman. Each one is elaborately adorned with some kind of ornament, a giant coffee pot, an enormous incense burner, one has a globe of the world on it, and others have mock traditional forts, traditional Omani fishing boats, arches and so on. It makes for very pleasant viewing and driving. The roads and their verges are immaculate, grass as smooth and verdant as any English bowling green. Potted flowers line the edge of this grass. Muscat is said to be one of the most beautifully kept and clean capitals in the world. All of this done by a veritable army of immigrant labour from the Indian sub-continent.

And so we leave the province of Muscat and Seeb behind us and enter the Batinah coast, the most fertile area of Oman. The beautifully kept roadside gardens disappear to be replaced by scrubland, yet a few hundred yards away one sees the tops of date trees in plantations where other crops are grown that are brought daily to the street markets where villagers gather daily to exchange wares and news. News and tales play a great part in the lives of Omanis; they are very much a race of oral tradition where stories from other individual hamlets and villages are related only to be brought back and shared over evening supper. At night in the villages all over Oman, after Magreb, the sunset prayers, the villagers will all return to their houses and the families will sit around one large platter of food, which they will all share and each member, from the youngest to the oldest will dispense his tales of the day, the story of his or her life on that particular day: the children will talk about what happened at school; the wife will talk about who she met at the market while buying the dinner; the husband about his day at work; the grandfather about the strange visitor to the village that day who arrived as he and his friends were outside the house drinking coffee. There will be no pregnant pauses, just a great desire on the part of the individual to relate his tale and feel complete as an integral part of that family unit.

Forty kilometres outside of Muscat we arrive at a small township by the name of Barka. Barka played a very important part in Omani history for it was here that a great battle was fought by Ahmed bin Said Al-Busaiidi, the first Sultan under the Al-Busaiidi dynasty that to this day governs Oman, and liberated Oman from Persian influence in 1744. Since then no foreign power has invaded or occupied Oman.

The dynasty that governed before the Al-Busaiidi dynasty was the Al-Yaruba dynasty which presided over Oman from 1624 to 1743. These years were heady years for Oman; they saw the creation and expansion of the Omani Empire. Oman was a seat of great learning, arts and sciences. Indeed Abu Ubaida bin Al Qassim was responsible for the beginnings of the science of marine navigation and made the seven thousand kilometre voyage from Oman to Canton, China, which eventually became a major trading route. However earlier in Omani history, another power was to threaten Oman.

In 1507, after realising the extent and wealth of the Omani Empire, the Portuguese invaded Oman and took control of the most important strategic trading ports of Sohar, Muscat, Qalhat, Hormuz and many other ports along the coast. All along the coast one finds fine examples of Portuguese forts but none as fine as the two in Muscat that overlook the harbour. The Portuguese did not venture inland, remaining on the coast. However it was from inland, Rustaq, that Nasser bin Murshid Al-Yaruba in 1624 sent a large army to attack the Portuguese in Muscat and such attacks as these continued for nearly one hundred years, gradually eroding the Portuguese defences. Eventually, at the end of the Al-Yaruba dynasty, a substantial amount of ships were assembled that defeated the Portuguese and rid Oman finally of their influence.

And so we continued our journey up the Batinah coast, Jassim and I, our conversation flowing without the awkward pauses one sometimes experiences with strangers when chatting. It struck me that Omanis would not have any problems in conversing with anyone: they are by nature garrulous, inquisitive and spontaneous and seemed to have a wonderful sense of humour. I was beginning to find myself very relaxed in Oman and in the company of Omanis, and as our conversation continued uninterrupted the small villages of the Batinah coast sped by. In all Arab countries the first name of a child is given but the second name must be of the father that sired this child; this includes women, and the third name is that of the grandfather. Maternal or paternal grandfather you ask.

Jemmil, a good friend of mine, an Omani, and myself were going out one evening. However before we went out we drove his wife and children to her village so she could stay with her parents. It was dusk; the roads just desert tracks. The village was about fifteen minutes' drive away and when we arrived at the house two women came to the car, one obviously the mother of Jemmil's wife the other lady much older. When we left the village I asked Jemmil who was the older lady.

"Oh, that was my wife's grandmother."

"Ah," I said.

But then he added, "She is my grandmother also."

It then dawned on me that, as it is tradition in Oman to marry your first cousin, then you will share the same grandparents. In Oman it is very unusual to marry outside the family and the norm is to marry one's first cousin, and many of these marriages are arranged when the children are born. However it is important to mention that the marriages though arranged are not forced, so that if two cousins do not get on they will not be forced to marry; rather they will look to find a cousin with whom they do get on and as the Omani families are large this invariably happens. Statistically the marriages are very successful, in that the divorce rate is very low. I suppose that this can be attributed to many factors: the large extended family units that help sort out disagreements etc., the fact the couples are not totally dependent on each other exclusively. Jemmil was later to become an important figure and great friend in my life in Oman and it was through him that I learnt many of the ways of the Omanis and got access to what had previously been an unknown culture. I was to meet his wife, his father and the entire family. I would be a frequent visitor at his house and eventually become a neighbour, and Jemmil was to help me through one of the darkest episodes of my life.

"What about the different turbans the Omanis wear, does that signify anything?" I asked Jassim.

"You can usually tell which of the eight regions of Oman someone comes from by the way he wears his turban and by the mixture of colours. For example," he continued, "a lot of people from the interior do not wear turbans at all; also in Muscat they wear kumas: that small skull-like hat that is also worn by many in Africa." Ah, I think, yet another remnant of Oman's glorious past.

After about one hundred and twenty kilometres, we turn right at a roundabout and believe it or not there was a traditional Omani fishing boat sitting on it. We drive for a couple of kilometres, come to a military checkpoint and enter the Naval Base at Wudham. It was while working here for the next four years that I was to become immersed in a culture of great riches and where I was to learn a lot about life, myself and my part in the great cosmos of life.

MUSICAL NIGHTS

I was shown to my room on the Naval Base. I was brought there by an Indian steward. It was a concrete villa, with ceiling fans and air conditioners, a large kitchen, dining room and lounge with a patio, a garden at the end of which was a wall and beyond that wall the sea. I proceeded to unpack, after which I lay on the bed and watched the ceiling fan whirr around. I was reminded of the opening scene in *Apocalypse Now* with Martin Sheen in some sleazy hotel room somewhere in downtown Saigon. I soon fell into a troubled afternoon sleep that featured helicopters, Wagner's "The Ride of the Valkeries" and Robert Duvall's "I love the smell of napalm in the morning". Thankfully I was awoken from this Dante's inferno type dream by a loud knocking at the door. It was one of my flat mates. By then, I noticed, it was dark.

"Fancy a pint?" he said.

"Do I ever," I replied.

Dave was his name. "You can't go into the Officers' Mess dressed like that," he said. I looked at myself in wrinkled jeans and shirt, unshaven and probably smelly from the sweat that had oozed out of me during my nap. "I'll give you fifteen minutes," he said. So I showered, shaved and changed and began to look human.

"Right then," said Dave, "let's go." Dave was quite a large chap with a shock of unruly red hair and with a ruddy complexion whose family name was Kavanagh. He did not look unlike a cattle farmer from Mullingar in Ireland. I could picture him in his Wellingtons and a flat cap, wielding a stick and driving cattle through muddy green fields, opening and closing gates behind him, supping pints of Guinness at the bar, perched on a stool, in a dimly lit, heavily teaked, smoky pub in the Irish Republic. Thirty seconds later we were at the Officers' Mess Bar, the first in.

"Where are you from Dave?" I asked as we were sipping our first pint.

"Swindon," he replies. Oh well so much for my intuition. Dave himself had only just arrived in Oman. He was good company and I could see that we would have no problem getting along. The Officers' Mess was like some museum piece from a period movie. There were old rifles on the wall and Indian stewards running around attending your every need, serving drinks on silver trays. White wine was brought in ice buckets. A couple of chaps in uniform were in the snooker room. The floors were marble scattered with oriental rugs. Omani stewards were also evident in their white dishdashas, cummerbunds and turbans, beaming smiles and serving food; what they lacked in their linguistic skills they certainly made up for in their exotic appeals and their politeness. "You are welcome" was the sum total of their linguistic talents.

"Thank you, you are welcome"; "You have brought me the wrong dish I am afraid"; "You are welcome"; "This chicken is still pink"; "You are welcome"; "The goat you served me is still alive"; "You are welcome." And so it all began at Wudam. Opposite the bar was the reading room. This was frequented solely by the British expatriates as it was an unwritten rule that there was only hush inside. The Omani officers wouldn't dare go in there. Unable to be quiet for more than fifteen seconds, they avoided it as if it contained some horrible contagious disease from which they would never recover.

As the drinks went down so too did the bar fill up, slowly at first but by nine o'clock it was heaving. There was a good mix of Omani officers and English teachers drinking plus a few British officers.

Here I feel I should mention Bernie Bruen, at one time the most decorated man in Britain's Armed Forces. He was in bomb/mine disposal and served in the Falklands. His legendary status was secured when while on a ship dismantling a bomb that had failed to go off, he took a break, fetched his violin, which of course he referred to as his fiddle, and with legs astride the bomb he began to play; and so a legend was born. Luckily the first night I was in the bar Bernie arrived and had brought his fiddle with him. In tow was Jeremy, a young fresh-faced sub lieutenant, who had also just arrived and who played the whistle. Jeremy was blond, blue eyed and terribly public school, all cricket jerseys, white flannels, rugby shirts and first eleven. A nice chap nonetheless. It was apparent that Bernie had taken young Jeremy under his wing. An Omani by the name of Salim, in traditional dress, appeared carrying an Oudh. This is an Arabic type guitar. So it looked as though we were in for an evening of music, Western meets Middle Eastern. Traditional sea shanties and traditional Arabic romantic songs about unrequited love, added to that some famous pub songs, "Wild Rover", "Whisky in the Jar". By this time everyone was singing in all languages: everyone possessed the gift of tongues. Rather like an evangelist, born-again, revivalist movement only with lots of wine. Towards the end of the night Salim started to play his Oudh again, this time the Arab answer to the Irish reel. At this young Jeremy got up and did the Dance of the Seven Veils and was an absolute natural; he had obviously had a lot of practice in the dorms of public school. It was such a good night that nobody wanted to leave, so nobody did. The senior officer present declared an extension until 2a.m. and the music and the fun continued.

I walked outside the bar onto the patio and looked up to a veritable canopy of stars glittering in the clear black sky. A shooting star rushed across this canvas and beyond the Mess garden one could hear the waves of the Indian Ocean gently lapping onto the shore. I felt so lucky and content to be here and to experience this. I thought to myself I must have been good to someone, somewhere along this journey through life.

TIME TO MOVE

After three months of living on the Naval Base I was beginning to feel a little institutionalized and I also wanted to experience life in the local community in one of the villages. I was eventually to move fifteen times. However, I will never forget my first house. It was located in Wudham Sahel. Sahel, in Arabic, means on the coast. I was to move to a small fishing village about five kilometres from the Naval Base. By now I had made quite a few local Omani friends. When I told my pals of my plans to move out and live off the base they were all for it and set about looking for a suitable place.

It was winter time in Oman. That is about 24 degrees Celsius, and I was to move into a house that had only just been built and I was to be the first occupier of this dwelling. The house itself had no air conditioners but did have ceiling fans that were perfectly adequate for the time of year. The village itself was a very traditional Omani fishing village, primitive in that there were no made-up roads, only dusty tracks, with goats wandering all over the village eating anything and everything. The local inhabitants seemed to be engaged in nothing more strenuous than walking from one neighbour's house to another – a laid-back existence. Even the fishermen seemed to spend most of their time sitting around on the beach, mending their nets, leaning against their boats whiling away the time with what for me were incomprehensible tales. Perhaps they went fishing late at night or early in the morning. In fact this is exactly what they did.

Early one morning I got up and drove along the coast; the fishermen were casting their nets onto the still waters and I thought back to biblical times, when Jesus recruited his disciples from such men as these. There is spirituality about this whole region of deserts and mountains and fishing villages that permeates the whole being. The Omanis in the village were very friendly and welcoming and not fearful of strangers at all. All in all it seemed ideal. At weekends Omani friends would come around and we would sit, and watch a movie. I remember on one occasion, I and an Omani were watching the movie *Excalibur*: wizards, witches, magic, spells – all of this genre fascinated the Omanis. While we were watching the movie Hamed asked me at what period of time Merlin was around. I guessed and said about 1200 years ago. "Really," he said, "did they have television at that time?" He obviously thought the film was a kind of documentary shot at the time of Merlin's life. Such was the simplicity of these people that I had forgotten that until 1970 there were only ten kilometres of black-top road, the rest were tracks and passes. There was no television, radio, electricity. There was one hospital in all of Oman with just twelve beds. Oman was certainly a land that time forgot until very recently and even now there is something of that psyche remaining in the people. It is refreshing, a kind of innocence unspoilt by the evil, worldly ways of the modern world. There is a sense of being in the Garden of Eden before the forbidden fruit was consumed. The men and women here have the beautiful simplicity of children and that so attractive naivety that we in the West seem to have lost somehow and somewhere along the way. Maybe the forbidden fruit is that of materialism and or capitalism. The Bedu does not collect possessions; he is neither acquisitive nor envious. If he has enough food for his family and his livestock, that is sufficient for him, he can then spend his time talking with his neighbours, exchanging news, drinking coffee and eating dates. This is when he is happy and all is right with the world. "Al-Hamdillilah", (thank God) he will say or "Allah Kareem", (God is good/kind).

In my new house in Wudham life was proceeding smoothly and I was integrating into the local community and experiencing life in Oman.

From now on I had very little contact with the ex-pats. When Hamed left that night after being mesmerized by Merlin's antics in *Excalibur* I went to bed. However I was awoken at 2a.m. in the morning by a banging, like someone hammering in the bathroom. I got up to investigate but as I approached the bathroom the hammering stopped. I thought little about it and went back to bed and straight to sleep. Yet this was to be the beginning of a series of strange happenings that were to take place in my house over the next few weeks. "There are more things, Horatio…"

The following week this hammering continued and began to worry me somewhat. Also at night wild dogs would run around the perimeter of the house howling and baying at the moon. At the weekend I decided to have a party. Some Omani friends came to my place. I was telling the assembled gathering about the goings on with the hammerings and the dogs etc. The Omanis glanced at each other in a knowing non-verbal way. The layout of the house was such that when you entered you were faced with a long hall, to right of which were all the living quarters, first the lounge, then the two bedrooms; at the end of the hall was the bathroom and to the left of that was the kitchen. Later on that night Hamed and the others went into a deadly hush. "Don't you hear anything?" said Hamed.

"No," I replied, telling him I was quite hard of hearing and had been since birth.

"Well," he said, "I, Mubarrak, Juma and the rest of us have been listening to whispering in the corridor." They were all slightly unnerved. Just then the feral dogs began their nightly tour of running around the house, howling and baying at the moon.

Juma then said, "They do not want you here, Rory, they do not want you living here."

"Who doesn't?" I asked Juma.

"Whoever was here before you."

"But there was no one here before me; I am the first one to live here." Juma just shrugged his shoulders enigmatically.

So the weekend passed and the following week the hammering in the bathroom continued and so too did the dogs continue their nightly circuit. One night around 2a.m., the hammering intensified in its momentum and whenever I approached the bathroom it would stop. However as soon as I was to return to bed it would start again. I became nervous, jumped into the car and drove back to the Naval Base where I spent the night in my room in the villa, which I still retained.

I was determined not to leave my house in the village, as I had made it comfortable and furnished it and the thought of finding another place and going through the moving process again was not very appealing. About one week after I had passed that night on the Naval Base, I left for work from Wudam Sahel at about 6.30a.m. I remember it well, by now the weather was heating up and it would soon be time to install air conditioning units. At about 10a.m., the temperature was early thirties Celsius and climbing. The staff on the base were asked to produce their military ID cards for inspection. I had left mine in the house in the bedroom on the side table. I went back to the house to collect it and on entering the bedroom I felt as if I were walking into a freezer. I could see my breath being exhaled; it was ice cold in there and no air conditioning. The hairs on my back rose up: I was goose pimpled all over and freezing. I grabbed my ID card and ran out of the house into my car and made my way back to the base. As I was driving I began to experience this strange mental aberration: I had no idea where I was in the world. I was trying to work out if I was in Saudi, Kuwait or Bahrain; all of these countries I had worked in previously. This confusion lasted until I was faced with the security police at the gate of the Naval Base.

I was never to return to that house again except to go and retrieve my belongings.

Soon after I had moved from Wudham Sahel, one of its residents informed me that the house I had occupied had been left empty for quite a considerable time before I moved in. When I asked him why, he replied, "Oh, didn't you know? That house was built on an old burial site and people were superstitious about moving in…" Juma was right; they did not want me to live there.

THE BEDU OF THE SHARQIYAH

So reluctantly I took up residence on the Naval base again.

Until the 1970s the Omani was living in isolation; he had been living his way of life for generations, mostly pastoral, strongly spiritual and a far cry from the sacred cows of modern day capitalism, money and accumulation of as many goods as possible. Most goods in Oman were exchanged through a bartering system and currency was only one form of exchange. The Omani worked to live, he did not live to work and his family and religion were his two priorities; once he had taken care of these two he felt free to relax which he did by drinking coffee and talking with his friends. There was no TV or radio. They were not bombarded with capitalistic or materialistic propaganda; they were able to live their lives free from the pressures of possessing things, as were their children who were able to be children and swim in the wadis and play in the mountains and deserts at whatever games they wished. Oman is a land where children are free to be children and have a semblance of childhood. I wish that were so in the West, where from the earliest age children, through the media, are taught to want all the time; there is little spirituality and even fewer human values other than the ones that involve the acquisition of money and material goods.

I had by this time become a good friend of Juma. Juma was a Bedu from the Sharqiyah region of Oman. He was from one of the small villages that skirted a desert, known as the Wahiba Sands. He invited me to visit him in his village. I left the Navy and drove for four and a half hours. It was to be my first real trip, a real passage of rites, and a voyage of body and soul of epic proportions. When I arrived at Juma's house, he gave me coffee and fruit and then we took the four-wheel drive into the sands of the Sharqiya. I found it awe-inspiring. This desert would be a dream for film makers, indeed it resembles the Empty Quarter, part of which is in Oman and then crosses into Saudi Arabia. It was from southern Oman near Salalah that the explorer Wilfred Thesiger began his trip across the Empty Quarter, guided by Omani Bedu, described in his seminal book *Arabian Sands*. Large dunes feature in The Wahiba with fine sands. Desert tracks that are passable in the morning become impassable in the afternoon because of the desert breezes that cause a shift in the sands. The Bedu alone know which are passable and those that are treacherous. It is foolish to attempt even going a few kilometres into these sands without a Bedu to guide you there and back. It is easy to become disoriented and to lose one's way, or to get stuck in the sand. Several expatriates have lost their lives by going in alone only to be found only a few kilometres from the main road. It does not take long to die in the heat of the summer when the temperatures rise to the mid fifties and there is no shade.

Date plantations litter these villages that are veritable oases on the edge of a desert, all drawing their water from an underground source. The sun's rays slant through the palm trees to give a dazzling dappled effect of yellow light and greenery. Every corner you turn in these villages you will find a photograph that is waiting to be taken, whether it be the plantations, the old Bedu in traditional dress, the young man hitching a ride with a Lee Enfield rifle strapped across his shoulder, the covered girls and women buying vegetables from the market. Looking out to the desert plains one sees herds of goats being driven by women dressed from head to toe in black. The faces of the women are dark, lined, weathered and timeless; it is impossible to tell their respective ages. They seem oblivious to everyone and everything except for the slow march of their herds and the slow march of time.

Falajes are to be found in every village. These are underground water systems that irrigate the food crops. Built from these falajes are bathing houses that are underground. They are usually situated in convenient spots in the village where you will see a wall with three corners. On the fourth corner will be a series of steps that will take you about four metres underground. There you will see a rather fast running stream that has been divided into three or four cubicles. You will choose a free cubicle and, wearing shorts, sink into the water that is about three feet deep where you can submerge your whole body and bathe.

The peculiar thing about these falajes is that they contain many small fish that are like specially designed skin cleaners; they will come and nibble all parts of your body taking away all the dead skin and basically picking you clean, leaving you to feel wonderfully refreshed after your bath. Obviously there are separate falajes for ladies and before the introduction of showers in the house everyone would use the falajes to bathe. Even now they are still frequented by many villagers who prefer to take their daily bath in this fashion.

The area of Ghallan where Juma lived consists of two main townships, Bani Bu Ali and Bani Bu Hassan. Juma lived in the latter. I remember on my first trip to Ghallan I was riding in the passenger seat holding a rifle. Every Bedu owns a rifle and it is legal to do so even now. Often at the weekend in the village square you will find Bedu men gathered in a circle drinking coffee and eating dates while at the same time they are taking apart and cleaning their rifles: quite an extraordinary sight. While Juma and I were driving through the desert one night I heard the beating of drums. I asked Juma to stop the car and listened to this rhythm, slow and steady, only the drum beat accompanied by a high-pitch wailing in the darkness of a moonless night in the desert where only dancing shadows could be seen. "What is that, who are they, what are they doing?" I asked Juma.

"They are having a party; it is called a 'Soama'. It takes place in the desert, away from all, and on occasions the drums will beat through the night and they will dance till sunrise. That is all I know," he said as we got in the car and drove away, the drums still beating behind us as we left.

Bani bu Ali and Bani bu Hassan are quite typical Bedouin villages. Although these people were previously nomadic they have largely settled in the villages. However their spirit is still the spirit of the nomad in that they still spend as much of their free time in the desert as they can, where they also keep their livestock, goats and camels, and they usually build a small dwelling made from palm leaves. Camel breeding is big business in this area. Rich Arabs from all the Gulf States come here to purchase their racing camels. Oman is said to produce the finest racing camels in the world. It is a great sight to behold when the Bedu are training their camels and races are held with camels from different villages. The jockey will be a young boy of seven or eight years old and just after dawn, when the sun has risen, the race will begin. On both sides of the camel track four-wheel-drive pickups will follow the camel race, driving behind, yelling on words of encouragement to their own camels, leaving in their wake great clouds of dust, making it impossible to see the outcome of the race, unless you are fortunate enough to be in one of the pickups. It takes the jockey about two kilometres after the finishing line to stop his camel.

The relationship between a camel and its owner is very strong and close. In times of sickness the Bedu will sleep with his camel. I remember one time, when I was with Abdullah, a Bedu from the Dara region of Oman. We were taking a break from the desert and checked into a hotel in Abu Dhabi. While we were in the lobby Abdullah received a phone call from his father to tell him that his camel had gone into labour. Immediately Abdullah explained to me he had to go and help the camel through its birth and then he was off into the night on a five-hour drive so he could be with his camel to help her give birth. I must admit I thought all those stories about the Bedu and their camels were a myth until I experienced it firsthand. He returned after five days with a big smile on his face and said, "It's a boy."

Back in Ghallan, it is a visual feast driving around these villages seeing the Bedu wearing his turban in a distinctive fashion. It is usually worn tilted to one side, giving a sort of jaunty rakish effect, and the tassels are allowed to flow freely. Although to the casual observer the turban looks as if it has been thrown on in a haphazard way, in fact a great deal of time has been taken by the individual to achieve this effect. The driving here is very haphazard and the young men will drive around casually with the driver's knee perched on the window still while he steers the car with his elbow. The cars are rarely washed and usually covered with sand and dust from forays into the edge of the desert. One weekend that I was there I did not see a single car that did not have a cracked windscreen. The car is a tool; it has a function to perform and as long as this function is fulfilled there is no need for prettying up one's vehicle. In fact the basics of life are performed without attention to the trappings: food, shelter and all other things essential to life. A Bedu can and will sleep in the most basic of dwellings, or preferably under the stars. He will survive quite happily on a diet of rice and meat and bread. If you ask him what his favourite food is he will look at you in bewilderment and say meat and rice or fish and rice. The taste is not that important to the Bedu; he knows he has to eat to live and he does just that. His wife will not spend hours on a soufflé or a cordon bleu meal. As for someone being a vegetarian this was incomprehensible to the Bedu. I told Juma that I had a guest coming from England. Juma said you must bring him to my village. "I will," I replied, "but he does not eat meat."

"Is he a vegetable man," says Juma.

"Yes," I reply.

"No problem," says Juma, "we will give him chicken." The Bedu do not view chicken as proper meat, therefore it is eminently suitable for vegetable men. Another friend of mine, Pauline, came to visit and one weekend we went to Juma's village. Pauline spent the weekend with the women in the house and gardens. I did not see her the whole weekend; she was given handmade Omani women's clothing to wear and her hands and feet were hennaed. All these clothes were given to her as a present when she left; such is the generosity of the Omani. I went off with the men shooting and sleeping in the desert; it was the expected thing to do. The Bedu men and women have different roles to fill, different but equal. One Omani Bedu said to me, "Rory, the people from the West think we, the Bedu or Arab, treat our women as second-class citizens; that is not true. We liken our men and women to different flowers that grow in a garden, each flower has its own scent, different yet beautiful; who can say the scent of one flower is greater than the other. That is how we view our men and women, different flowers with different scents, neither more beautiful than the other, just different."

The morning that Pauline and I were to leave; Juma's younger brother came and brought a box saying it was a present for Pauline. Pauline thanked him, opened the box and inside was a snowy white rabbit. I said to Juma to thank his brother but there was no way that I could drive half way across Oman with a rabbit jumping around in the car. "No problem," said Juma, "if you cannot take the rabbit with you, you can stay a little while longer and we will have it for lunch." As you can imagine Pauline looked horrified, knowing that Juma was serious. Needless to say I did drive half way across Oman with a rabbit. However he did not jump around; he settled on the back seat, probably grateful in the knowledge that he had had a close shave and had managed to escape. He was not going to push his luck any further.

There is a sense of lawlessness and anarchy here that does not exist elsewhere in Oman. Yet this anarchy gives one a sense of freedom and of a being without constraint. Rousseau's "Noble Savage" comes to mind when looking at these Bedu, and they are noble and have not lost that primitive force inside. In Jungian terms their primitive psyche remains intact, that primeval power and urge that makes the Bedu so strong, so essential, individual, intuitive and spontaneous and above all it makes him so vital and impossible to control or rein in. This makes him the free spirit that deep down we all want to be.

In Bani Bu Ali stands probably the most fascinating mosque in Oman with a huge number of domes. Nobody knows exactly how old it is but it is thought to be around 1200 years old. The Omani belongs to a sect of Islam that is called Ibadhi; this is different from the Shia and Sunni sects and it is the most tolerant of all three.

On my first trip to Bani Bu Hassan Juma took me off to visit his uncles and grandfather. On entering the male majlis (Arabic for lounge, there will always be two majlis in an Omani household one for men and one for women) all the men stood up and I shook hands with them individually. We then sat down and great platters of fruit and dates with coffee were served. The coffee comes in very small cups and is very strong; it is considered polite to drink two cups. However after you have drunk your fill you have to shake the cup in your right hand to indicate you desire no more. If you do not do so the person who is serving the coffee, usually the son of the householder, will continue to pour you coffee. Juma was informing me of all this protocol while at the same time translating into Arabic our conversation to the assembled men. He told us one story that a while back a Westerner had arrived in the village and because he had not known about this custom had drunk vast amounts of unwanted coffee. On hearing what was required of him the Westerner sighed. After the coffee was served supper was provided. The supper usually is of meat and rice and eaten from one large platter by all. Having eaten his full the Westerner was encouraged to eat more whereupon he picked up the platter of food and began to shake it from side to side believing this was the custom to indicate you had had your fill; of course it was not and this anecdote sent the assembled gathering into roars of laughter.

Also a custom in Oman is that the host himself will serve you the choicest pieces of meat with his right hand; food is eaten with the right hand and no cutlery is used at all. The same applies to fruit; the host will slice apples, oranges and peel bananas and hand them to you. Because everything in this society is governed by strict protocol I was determined not to offend and accepted all I was offered. However it was after I had eaten the fifth banana I looked at Juma and said to Juma, "I can't eat any more bananas, I am not a monkey." Juma laughed out loud and translated to all whereupon they all burst into laughter.

The grandfather then said to Juma, who translated for me, "I was wondering how many bananas he was going to eat, I just kept feeding him to see when he would stop." The grandfather must have been ninety years of age but had a twinkle in his eye. He then proceeded to dunk his date into this viscous liquid. He invited me to do the same by saying it was good for the libido and he was looking for a new wife at the age of ninety. I accepted his offer, dunked my date and put it in my mouth. The liquid was warm and it tasted awful. I looked up to see all these Bedu watching me. Juma told me that the liquid was fresh oil from the cow's stomach. I have never tasted anything quite so disgusting and it took me all my effort to swallow this date without throwing up on the fruit platter. Needless to say there were whoops of laughter from the assembled men and I too joined in their mirth and was delighted at their sense of humour and enjoyment of life.

That night Juma and I slept outside in the desert, watched shooting stars and talking away about our lives and different customs. We eventually fell asleep to be woken at dawn by a glorious sunrise the like of which you can only experience by sleeping outside in the desert. The only real concession the Bedu have made to the modern world is to trade in their camel for four-wheel-drives for travelling, although some still prefer to travel by camel; other than that they remain as they always have been. This was to be the first of countless occasions that I was to sleep under the stars and awake to the desert sun. The Bedu themselves say that one day sleeping outside will give you more energy than four days sleeping in the house. I knew then that the Bedu are only really at home when they are spending their time in the desert. I awoke that morning feeling more alive than I have ever felt before. For the first time in my life I knew I was enjoying a life that was one of my own choice, not one that had been foisted upon me by Western society. I was at last set free from the chains of my Western education that had kept my mind in shackles for too long and I knew then that there would always be apart of me that would, in some measure, yearn for the for the life of the nomad of the desert.

THE TRUCIAL STATES

"Al-Hamdillilah," thank God. This is the reply given to you when you ask an Omani "How are you?" He could be in hospital, just suffering from a bereavement or generally unwell, however he will inevitably give you this answer when asked about his health. Unlike in the West where you will receive replies ranging from "ok", "fed up", "feeling awful", "really depressed" and a litany of other negative replies. In the old adage, "is a glass half full or half empty?" – Well for the Omani it is always half full and to think otherwise would be to fly in the face of God as life could be much worse. One of my Omani acquaintances had just died and I rang his family to express my sorrow, "How are you all?" I said. "Al-Hamdillilah," was the reply I received. This at one time shocked me and yet in the same instant filled me with admiration for the Omani, for his acceptance of the inevitable and despite the great sorrow the great dignity with which the Omani accepted his misfortune.

Abdullah's brother has just been admitted to hospital for a serious operation. "How is everything Abdullah?"

"Al-Hamdillilah," he replied. This is the Abdullah who rushed back from Abu Dhabi to help his camel through her labour and was so delighted at the birth of a boy camel. Abdullah came from the area known as Dara, the most sparsely populated region of Oman, populated largely by Bedu; its capital city is Ibri. Abdullah and Juma were both Bedu; despite the fact that they were from different tribes and different regions they had a lot in common and became very good friends. It was through Juma that I met Abdullah and soon we were to become inseparable, travelling the whole area of Oman in four-wheel-drive vehicles. We drove through deserts, mountains, wadis, never sleeping indoors, always sleeping under the stars. There is a great amount of personal freedom in Oman. You can pull off a main road and drive a mile into the desert and camp, and nobody will bother you, no police to tell you that camping is allowed only in designated areas. In fact at night if a vehicle did approach us Juma and Abdullah would walk away from where we were camped, holding their rifles, greetings would be changed with the visitors, and in as nice a way as possible the visitor would be asked what he wanted. It is quite common for whole families to camp outside, women and children, and any approaching vehicle to their choice of camp ground could be a potential threat to the families, and if vehicles do approach they do so at their own peril.

Abdullah told us a story that near his village a whole family were camping out in the desert, not too far from the road. A police vehicle decided to approach the family and when they got too close the Bedu opened fire and killed the policemen. One has to understand that although these people may have a house in a village skirting a desert they are still essentially Bedu: thousands of years of mental evolution cannot be changed in a generation. As it turned out this matter was taken to court and the Bedu were acquitted on the grounds that the police did not identify themselves, neither did they have reason to approach the family; there had been no shooting, no disturbance of the peace. Since then no desert area has been patrolled at night-time and very rarely in the daytime so you are free to travel and stop and sleep where you desire. This freedom, something taken for granted by the Bedu here, is a thing that Westerners put a great premium on and adds to the sense of freedom of spirit that is so wanting in the West. I sometimes wonder if the great consumption of drugs in the West is in fact a desire on the part of the individual to escape the total control that society has on his life and his soul and because of this is his inability to be spontaneous and intuitive. His life is one that has been programmed for him by the world in which he lives; he just wants to break free.

Ibri, capital of Dara, is not far from Al Ain, which is now part of the United Arab Emirates formerly The Trucial States, Trucial Coast, Trucial Oman. Up until the 1820s all of these Trucial Sates were part of the Omani Empire. However this area was notorious for its pirates and was dubbed "The Pirate Coast". These pirates were interfering with the British trade with India and so after several naval skirmishes between the British and the Omanis, the seven sheikdoms that make up the UAE were locked into a truce with Britain and Oman lost control over them. This truce was formalized in 1892 by a treaty made between Britain and the UAE. After World War Two the British granted internal autonomy to the UAE. However, Oman still retains control of Musandam, which sits on the narrowest part of the Arabian Gulf, opposite Iran, where 90% of the world's oils supplies flow, making Musandam one of the most strategically important pieces of land in the world.

Juma and I forged a bond, a bond that was to last for nearly ten years. At this time I was still residing on the Naval Base and Juma and Abdullah were also working there as sailors in the Royal Navy of Oman. It struck me as slightly incongruous that these Bedu who lived nowhere near the sea and spent as much time in the desert as possible would choose to work in the Navy. Neither Abdullah nor Juma could swim. In fact the only time that Abdullah was to go into the sea was when he was chosen, during a practice air to sea rescue mission, as the drowning man. He was winched from the ship, wearing a life jacket, and unceremoniously dumped into the rough seas; whereupon after several aborted attempts he was winched back up to the helicopter and then placed safely back on board. This experience terrified Abdullah and instilled a great fear of the sea into him. Needless to say Juma and I, with Abdullah, had many a good laugh at this whereupon Abdullah would retaliate and throw down the gauntlet challenging Juma at any time to a camel race. This was all done in good humour and the three of us were to know each other so well that on many occasions our frailties and idiosyncrasies were fair game for all.

I, for instance, could not change a wheel on my four-wheel-drive vehicle and whenever needed, Juma and Abdullah would do the necessary work. When a friend of mine once asked Juma why he would not teach me how to change a wheel, Juma replied that no way would he do so as then I would be fully independent of him and should we have a disagreement I could then drive off and be completely self-sufficient leaving him behind stranded.

There were occasions when we would have our disagreements, usually over which track to take when travelling through the mountains or the deserts. These would blow over for although the Bedu is hot blooded and will tend to flare up his anger will soon be forgotten. He does not bear a personal grudge and will not harbour anger and bide his time and wait for vengeance, Shakespeare's "Vengeance is a dish best eaten cold" does not apply to the Bedu, but does to those from the northern climes. So with my Irish blood and mercurial temper and the two hot-blooded Bedu there were times when things got heated, but the times were short-lived and probably necessary as a safety valve as we spent all our free time together and the inevitability of friction was always there. Having said that, a Bedu's first loyalty is to his family and tribe and should anyone attack his tribe or the honour of its people the Bedu will be swift in meting out revenge and will do so without mercy. However in a personal disagreement this was never the case. After some incident we would joke and try to imagine what the children would be like if an Irishman with his hot blood were to marry a Bedu woman. Would they be totally out of control?

I was later to learn that Juma and Abdullah joined the Navy purely and simply because it was the only job they could find and that their respective salaries were necessary to support the extended families in their villages. Unlike Saudi, Oman is not oil rich and unlike the United Arab Emirates it does not have a sound commercial base. So the Omanis, apart from the very few, are not a rich people, rather working class. I think in many ways this is their saving grace: they have their feet firmly on the ground; they are working class and this has kept them very much in touch with their own culture which has not been polluted by Western materialism. They are not really interested in acquisition of possessions with one exception, and that is a good four-wheel-drive car. The prince of four-wheel-drive vehicles in Oman is the Toyota Land Cruiser and all Omanis yearn for this as it is a superb off-road vehicle, probably the best in the world, and if you are driving in Oman you need a good off-road vehicle for some of the deserts are treacherous with their soft sand and the paths through the mountains can be tortuous and incredibly steep.

During the week, work time, we never slept on the base. We would meet in a car park on the Naval Base. In Omani society it is incredibly important that one is seen to be respectable and by the same token show respect. For this reason we would never drive off while the roads were empty as everyone was praying in the mosque; we would wait till evening prayers were finished, the mosques were emptied and people were going about their business. We would then drive off the Naval Base, stop in the local village and pick up some takeaway food, invariably meat or fish with rice and salad, then drive along a black-top road towards a town known as Rustaq.

Rustaq itself was a former capital of the Batinah region and possesses a beautiful fort, and is renowned throughout Oman for its crystal clear spring water that rises from a well adjacent to the main mosque. After twelve kilometres we would turn left into the desert and drive seven kilometres through the sands where we found an ideal place to camp. We were to camp in the same place for months on end. On reaching this particular spot we would unload the Jeep. A raffia mat would first be placed on the ground, then cushions spread around it and on the mat the food would be placed. The blankets for sleeping would be left in the car until it was time for sleeping. No fires were lit; one soon became accustomed to the night light. Bedu do not light fires in a camp unless it is for cooking. This is because in former days rival Bedu tribes and raiding parties could see lighted fires for miles. So fires were lit to cook breakfast after sunrise and before sunset to ensure safety of the family and tribe. Juma, Abdullah and I would eat and then turn to conversation about what had happened that day or really about anything that came to mind. Around 10p.m. we would sleep. Before that Juma would extricate three identical blankets from the Jeep. They were Navy issue. We would awake with the sunrise, reload the Jeep and return to the Naval Base to get ready for work. I remember not sleeping in a bed for three months. Those were glorious evenings, evenings where communications were from the soul and then suddenly, one night, in the same camping spot everything was to change.

POSSESSION

It was on another such evening, the same as any other, Abdullah and I were driving out to our camping ground. For some reason or other, I am not sure what, Juma was not with us. I think he was back in his village going through the courtship rituals of the Bedu with the woman he was soon to marry. Abdullah and I arrived in our same spot and began unloading the Jeep. When the task was finished and we were sitting on the mat, I began to feel uncomfortable, disturbed, unsettled for some reason. I looked towards the desert scrubs that were a few metres away from where we slept and swore I saw shadows flitting from one desert scrub bush to another. They were always seen out of the corner of my eye and when I tried to focus these shadows centre-on they would again flit away. I said nothing to Abdullah about this. I felt fear, irrationally so, yet nonetheless it was there. I said to Abdullah, "Come on, let's pack up we are going." He did not ask why, just proceeded with me to load the vehicle.

Half way through packing up he turned to look at me and said, "I know, Rory, I saw them too." We quickly finished our loading in complete silence, jumped into the car and I drove as quickly as I could from that spot. As I was driving through the desert I am sure I saw these same shadows jumping from desert scrub to desert scrub; they were chasing us of that I am sure. I looked at Abdullah whose face seemed frozen with fear. Neither of us spoke a word. I was determined to reach the black-top road as soon as possible and get out of the desert. It was then that I felt only what I can describe as being whacked around the head with an invisible baseball bat. I felt stunned as I drove along. A stretch of desert that was so familiar to me before had completely changed. Abdullah and I were now in a totally different part of the desert. This area I had never driven before and still the shadows were leaping from bush to bush. I was in a state of panic swinging the Jeep this way and that, desperately trying to escape these fleeing shapes and desperate to find a way out of the desert onto the black-top road. The Jeep was getting bogged down in soft sand. I changed into low gear and we scrambled out of a sand depression onto firmer sand. I swung to my left only to see a perimeter fence barring our entrance to the black top surface. This perimeter fence had never been there before. I steered the Jeep towards it and drove parallel with the fence hoping to find a gap somewhere; meanwhile I was aware of still being chased. Finally I saw what looked like a tear in the wire mesh and decided it was my only chance; I swung the car around and pointed her at this tear, deciding whatever happened I would drive the Jeep into the fence. I drove and luckily with some scraping and scratching got through the fence and onto the black-top road. The relief was immense. Abdullah said nothing. He did not have to. He had undergone the same experience as me. We drove back to the Naval Base in complete silence. I dropped him off at his room and then went back to sleep in my own. Little did I realize that the real horror had not yet even begun.

The next morning I got up for work as usual. Starting time was seven o'clock, yet from nine till ten we had a breakfast break. It was at this time that I chose to return to the camp site where the night before something inexplicable had happened. I had not spoken to Abdullah about the incident; he was at work somewhere down on the harbour, out of range of any telephone, However he was not on my agenda; for some inexplicable reason I felt the need to return to this place. I felt angry about what had happened the previous night, something or someone had chased me away, some act of incomprehensible violence had been perpetrated on me and I wanted to get my own back.

I went to the staff car park, got in my Jeep and started to drive. It was hot at that time but I felt neither hot nor cold, just driven by anger and a desire and lust for revenge. I found the camping spot easily enough. It somehow looked different in the daylight. The clearing where we usually lay our mat was surrounded on all sides by desert shrubs leaving about two square metres of clear camping area where we had been the night before. It was in those shrubs that I had seen the shadows jumping from bush to bush. I felt angrier and angrier. I knew what I was going to do, as if an inner voice were speaking to me telling me. My Jeep was full of rubbish, sandwich wrappers, empty food foil containers, coke cans, and a full ashtray. I had a desire to defile this place and that is exactly what I did. I emptied all the rubbish from the car into the desert area and rage drove me to scatter various pieces into the desert shrubs. It was a deed that I was to pay very gravely for and something I was forever to regret.

I remember very little of the rest of that day; nothing of great significance took place. Abdullah had gone back to his village for a week's holiday and I was later to discover that he had telephoned Juma and told him what had happened. As for myself that night I decided to stay on base as my two companions were gone and I did not relish another incident like the one that had happened the previous night. I had a few drinks in the Officers' Mess, went to bed, slept, got up and got ready for work in the morning.

That was when it happened; as I opened the door to let myself out I was gripped by an inexplicable panic. Frozen with fear, I could not move, I really did not want to leave the villa. I closed the door, went back inside and told myself that this was ridiculous. What on earth was going on? I never at any of the earlier stages connected my experience in the desert with what I was then feeling. I had another cup of tea and willed myself to leave this house and go to work. I got into my car to drive and I looked at my hands that were violently shaking. Eventually I inserted the ignition key and drove off. At the time I was teaching in a Portacabin down in the harbour; as I remember there were six naval radar trainees who needed help with their technical English. I duly arrived on time, entered the Portacabin and sat down. I looked up at these trainees and felt their eyes pressing into mine. I said nothing, I was incapable of speech, and I just stared at each of them with blankness.

"What is wrong?" they said.

"Nothing," I replied, "I do not feel well." Again I had this feeling of panic; I had to leave this place and so I did, I just upped and left them. I struggled to get back in my car and wondered what was happening to me. I drove straight to the Medical Centre and saw the Naval doctor, Chris, a friend of mine. I explained to him my symptoms. By now I was experiencing severe headaches.

He lay me down, took my blood pressure and gave me a cursory examination. "Your blood pressure is well over the safety margins," he said, "what has happened to you?"

"Nothing," I said, as I still could not connect the two incidents. He gave me some valium to calm me down, some sleeping tablets, and something to bring down the blood pressure, told me to go home and come and see him the following morning.

I did just as he asked me to and dutifully returned the following morning. My condition was worse. I had deteriorated badly, I was shaking, sweating and gripped with fear. My headaches were even more severe and as he took my blood pressure again he looked at me with telling eyes. "I am going to refer you to the hospital today," he said. "You will need a full scan." I cannot remember the technical terminology of the scan required but when I asked him if this were a brain scan he nodded.

I have always had a fear of hospitals and the thought of going for a brain scan only worsened my already fragile state. "No, doctor, let's wait until tomorrow; give me some more valium, I will go home and come back and see you tomorrow and if my condition has not improved then I will go to hospital." He reluctantly agreed and dispensed more medication.

I arrived home, swallowed the valium with some hot tea and lay on the sofa staring out of the window. It was then that it all fell into place. For some reason, maybe the effect of the valium, I saw the chain of events as exactly that: a chain that had led to my present condition. Was it possible, I asked myself, could this really happen to me in the twentieth century? Yet my intuition told me that it was possible and that what was wrong with me was not medical; it had to do with what had happened that night in the desert and my actions the subsequent day.

Jemmil told me that his father was a very important, highly respected exorcist and that Arabs from Saudi Arabia, Dubai, Doha and all the Gulf States would come and see him if they thought one of their family were possessed by evil jinn. (Jemmil had also told me that out of the five sons his father had it was Jemmil who had the "gift" and his father wanted to train him to become an exorcist; however Jemmil told me he had informed his father that he had no desire to do so.)

This possession would manifest itself in physical illnesses and nightmares, lethargy and panic attacks. Many wealthy Arabs would visit Jemmil's father after Western medicine had failed to cure one of their family. Jemmil's father never charged for his services and lived in a very humble abode in a house next to Jemmil's. I was never to go into Jemmil's paternal home and this was unusual. However I digress. Jemmil's father would have a consultation with the apparent victim of possession and would instantly tell the family whether this was a genuine case of possession or a malady that could be cured by Western medicine. If it were the former he would treat the patient; if the latter he would recommend that they take the medicine of the West. All this was going through my mind as I lay there with the calming effects of the valium. I began to think about the situation logically. What had really led up to my present condition? I was happy with my social life, my work; I was not stressed out for any reason. The more I thought about it the more convinced I became that the incidents on that day in the desert, my reaction to it and my present state of mind were somehow connected. I knew that there was only one way to find out. I picked up the phone and dialled a number. A woman answered and I said, "I would like to speak to Jemmil, please…"

THE EXORCISM

"Hi, Rory, how are you?" says Jemmil.

"Fine, well, not really," I replied and so I related all the events to Jemmil. He listened without interruption. Finally I told him what the doctor had said. Jemmil told me he would speak with his father and call me later. I waited anxiously for that phone call and when it finally came I grabbed the receiver and said, "Yes, tell me, Jemmil." Jemmil told me he had told his father about the incident and his father had asked Jemmil to bring me to his village that night after evening prayers. He said his father would talk to me but could promise me no help; however he would be able to tell whether I was indeed possessed and needed exorcism or whether my illness was one that could only be treated by Western medicine.

So I waited patiently and after sunset, still gripped by panic, drove to Jemmil's village. At night it looked like one would expect an ancient Arabian village to look like: single storey dwellings, dusty roads that disappeared into labyrinths of dusty tracks. Men and women like ghosts moving in and out of the shadows of their doorways. I arrived at Jemmil's house where his father was waiting. A small man with grey/black receding hair and a tuft of white beard on his chin. He was wearing a long white jellaba and invited me to sit down with him and tell him my tale again in my own words. Jemmil was our translator. I told him everything and from time to time watched his eyebrows rise. I told him about how I went back the following morning to the same place and emptied the rubbish from my car. It was at that point the expression on his face really became grave. He asked me to leave the room while he spoke to Jemmil. Jemmil eventually came outside and I looked at him anxiously. He said he a sombre voice, "My father says you are possessed by the jinn of the place that you defiled. The jinn were travelling through the spirit world and resting in that particular spot where you and Abdullah happened to camp. They chased you away as a warning, but you returned and desecrated their home, that is why they are in you. Abdullah is not sick because he did not take part in this defilement, but you are and if you do not receive treatment you will become sicker and die. My father has agreed to perform an exorcism on you."

I felt a great sense of relief. I was right; this was the cause of my illness. My inner voice had been vindicated and most important of all I was to be treated. I had at that time, and still now, no doubt as to the veracity of this diagnosis. Jemmil told me I would have to spend the next week with him in his house in the village so that his father could perform the exorcism and then monitor my condition. I drove back to the Navy, informed my colleagues to inform work that I had to go away to Britain on compassionate leave and then packed a few things and drove to Jemmil's house.

The next morning Jemmil's father came to the house and told me to take him to the exact spot in the desert where this incident had taken place. He was carrying with him a small canvas bag. We drove to the place in the desert and got out of the car. The desert midday sun burnt down on us. With Jemmil I was placed in the centre of the clearing. Jemmil's father then walked over to the bushes and walked a full circle around me muttering incantations. "What is he saying, Jemmil?" I asked.

"Oh, he is quoting verses from the Koran."

In four corners the father placed some twigs and straw and over each of these four piles he poured some rice. When he had finished with these four piles he set fire to each one in turn. He had a small clay frankincense burner and lit some frankincense. I was to stand completely still. He came to me and through Jemmil he asked me my mother's maiden name; I told him Valentine. He then started his incantations, walking around the circle and fires he had made with the incense burning and the smoke rising into the desert sky. He then came to me and held the incense pot so that the smoke travelled up my neck into my face and then into my hair. He stood next to me and called to the jinn in Arabic. Jemmil was translating for me. He was saying, "Oh listen to me, spirits of the air and ground, this son of Valentine did come to this place meaning no harm, he is not of these parts and does not know of our ways. He is sorry for his defilement of this place and asks you to forgive him and leave his body so he may be well. He will never desecrate a place where the jinn reside again. For the sake of his mother and God please leave him." He continued for a while and I was led into a kind of trance with the incantations, the desert sun, the smell of frankincense all around me, the fires burning in the corner, when suddenly Jemmil awoke me from this state and said the exorcism was finished. We left this place and drove back to the village. Jemmil explained on the way back that I was to stay with him and in the morning his father was to visit me and make sure the exorcism had been successful. In his father's view he thought it was to be a success. As things turned out this was not to be the case.

The following morning I awoke in a state of confusion. It took me a while to realize what had happened the previous day and also to realize where I was. For when we returned from the desert Jemmil took me to the male majlis where I lay on the cushions. He gave me a blanket and I fell into a deep sleep that would carry me through till the following morning. Jemmil came in with strong Omani coffee and breakfast of eggs, tomatoes and bread. I managed the coffee, yet I had no stomach for the food at all. He asked me how I was; I told him I felt no different. I was still in the grip of fear and by this time the thought of leaving the sanctuary of the room filled me with dread.

I gave Jemmil the blanket, sat up and vacantly stared at the ceiling fan. Ten minutes later Jemmil returned with his father; his father looked at me, said something to Jemmil and left. Jemmil told me what I already knew: the exorcism had not worked. His father had returned to his own home and was to work on some further treatment. For two days I remained in a fugue type state. I rarely spoke, just gazed at the ceiling, my mind blank, fixed on my own particular space in time, unable to move. During this time visitors came and went to the majlis. They were friends of Jemmil and were briefed on the situation, their reaction to which was one of complete acceptance; it was something they had all seen before, and before long it was as if I was not even in the room.

Everyday Jemmil's father would visit and leave shaking his head. I was not eating, just drinking water and sitting in the room all day. On the third day Jemmil's father arrived carrying in one hand a bottle that contained a viscous liquid in which there seemed to be twigs, flowers and all sorts of ingredients. In his other hand he carried a small package covered in newspaper. He spoke to Jemmil for a few minutes and then left. Jemmil then told me that inside the package was a special kind of frankincense and this I was to burn twice a day, once at sunset and once at sunrise. I was to place the burning clay pot on the ground and stand astride it naked so the smoke would rise up through my whole body. The liquid I was to drink also twice daily after I had performed the ritual with the frankincense. I obeyed like an automaton and after three days began to feel better. I no longer was possessed by this fear. I could go out without panicking and drove to the villages to accompany Jemmil shopping. I was definitely on the mend and felt such gratitude to Jemmil and his father. His father beamed when he saw me and said that I must finish all the frankincense and drink the liquid and then I would be fine.

A week had nearly passed and I was due back at work in a few days so I felt strong enough to return to the Naval Base. When I was leaving, Jemmil's father came and wished me well. I told him my gratitude knew no bounds; he told me that I was welcome, but through Jemmil he also explained to me that although the jinn had departed I would experience certain residual symptoms, particularly at night and almost certainly through dreams. He said that once one had been possessed there would forever be part of their soul that was tainted and that I should sleep with a copy of the Koran next to me. I asked him what form these symptoms would take but he was not forthcoming. However it was not to be too long before I was to find out exactly what he had meant.

I returned to the Naval Base and finished my treatment. It was after a few weeks that I began to experience these residual effects that Jemmil's father had told me about. They would always happen just as I was drifting off to sleep. I would feel a presence at the foot of the bed slowly crawling up from the bottom of the bed under the blanket. I would feel its hand around my feet trying to pull me under; gradually it would climb further up the bed and try to pull me under. I felt as if I were going to suffocate and desperately tried to move; however my body was paralyzed, frozen. I was gasping for air and, just as I felt I had taken my last breath, I would be able to move and switch on the bedside lamp and shake this sleep off me and with it this demon would disappear. This happened every night. I told Jemmil who in turn told his father. His father said this was to be expected. Alternatively I was told that these demons would not come if I had been drinking at all. Consequently my alcohol consumption did rise considerably and I felt justified in believing it was for medicinal purposes.

These nightly terrors did diminish in frequency, however even now they will occur and since my exorcism I have dreamt very deeply and vividly; sometimes these dreams have been nightmares and sometimes inexplicable vision like dreams. A few years later I came across the term the Incubus, which I looked up in the Oxford Dictionary: "A demon that comes at night... a person or thing that oppresses like a nightmare". I was later to learn that in Africa and primitive tribes, the presence of incubus and the experiences of this sleep death were common in people deemed to be possessed.

UNDER ARABIAN SKIES

After this my life became a little quieter for which I was truly grateful. Juma and Abdullah had gone off on naval exercises and would be away for a few months. In the meantime I was living on the Naval Base. However, after a short time I was to tire of expatriate life. I yearned for the intimacy of Omani village life and the open spaces, deserts and mountains, all out there waiting for me. Impetuously I rang Jemmil. I asked him if he could find me a house in his village that I could rent. He told me he knew just the place. The following weekend I was to move out, back to living in Oman again.

Jemmil arrived Thursday morning with a couple of pickup trucks. Thursdays and Fridays are the weekends throughout the Arab word, Friday being the Holy Day, our Sunday, where everyone goes to the mosque at about 12.30p.m. And there is the weekly sermon from the Imam, not unlike the Christian church on a Sunday. However, unlike Britain, the mosques are usually packed to overflowing and adult males are expected to attend Friday prayers. For the women it is an option, they may pray at home. On Thursday morning Jemmil, two of his Omani friends and I started the move into the village of Mulladda. It was inland about twenty kilometres from the coast: a typical Omani village. Once we had left the main road and entered the village, the roads were all unmade and dusty. We travelled through the village, past Jemmil's house and his father's, along past the local market where we stopped to buy some fruit. This was a wonderful scene, with old men riding donkeys; in fact donkeys were the principal transport carriers here, apart from our pickups, their produce was laid out on a mat on the desert floor: fruit, vegetables and ghet which was goat food and basically grass, the Arabic for grass (normal grass) is hashish. Fish was also on sale, and livestock, mainly goats. With the donkeys coming and going and people milling around in traditional clothing it looked like a biblical scene. The staple meat in most of Oman is goat and if you as an Omani receive any visitors from outside then it is incumbent on you to ask them to stay for lunch and to slaughter a fresh goat in their honour and then cook it. I always knew when Jemmil expected visitors as there would be invariably two goats tethered to a post outside his house. He often asked me to watch him slaughter them and always laughed at my squeamishness. When asked I would always think of Jodie Foster as Clarice Starling and Anthony Hopkins as Hannibal Lecter in *Silence of the Lambs*: "Can you still hear the lambs screaming, Clarice...?" All I could hear was the goats bleating yet a tingle still went up my spine.

On the road Jemmil told me a little about his village, well he knew only a little. As we drove through the village of Mulladda I saw these wonderful old mud brick houses of two or three storeys decaying. They looked like old merchant houses to me, but Jemmil said he did not know. There were also signs of very old settlements in the middle of the village, perimeter walls that you could only see the tops of. It was really an archaeologist's paradise and then suddenly my eyes nearly popped. We arrived in a clearing where there was a large fort, two thirds intact, and in one of the turrets there was an original cannon. I asked Jemmil to stop as I wanted to get out and take a photograph. I walked towards the fort, which was being occupied by goats, you will find goats everywhere in Oman, and climbed up to where the cannon was. I could not believe it; in England it would be a registered historical protected site. It looked like a Portuguese fort, but could have equally belonged to a tribal chieftain whose domain extended over large parts of this area.

I came back down and asked Jemmil how old that fort was. "It is quite old," he said, "I remember it being there when I was a kid." God I thought, these guys have no idea of the archaeological treasures that they are walking through. Maybe it is just as well. Perhaps all these links with the past just reinforce their collective unconsciousness, in Jung's term, and strengthen their sense of identity, of belonging and their place in the village and world in general; their village is their world.

We drove quite some way from the centre of the village, some five kilometres, and after fishtailing through a number of sandy tracks came to a rusted iron gateway. On the left of this was a small plantation growing dates and various other crops. On driving through the gate there was a clearing in which two large traditional Omani houses stood, one at the far end of the clearing. The other, that was to be mine, backed on to the walls of the plantation, a disadvantage as I was later to find out. The owner of the other house was also the owner of the plantation and he came out to greet us. We sat on the ground outside his house, drank coffee and ate dates and after a respectable lapse of time took our leave and went back to my house to unpack and check the house out. I was thrilled with it. It was surrounded by a concrete perimeter wall that led into a big dusty courtyard, with a few shrubs growing. I could see the potential with a bit of irrigation. The house was about twenty years old and made from breezeblock. It was quite solid. I entered the hallway and it was laid out again in traditional Omani fashion with a long hall and rooms off it. Outside to my delight there were outbuildings. They were like barns and I felt exhilarated to be in fact living in the Omani countryside, albeit not as green as England, but I had my plantation behind me, my outhouses; I felt like the Lord of the Manor and was so relieved to be away from the sterile life on the Naval Base.

Jemmil's two friends Saied and Salim were great fun. They carried all in laughing and joking as is the Omani way. After this, with Juma and Abdullah away somewhere sailing on the Arabian Sea, I was to spend a lot of time with Jemmil and his friends and gain access to a culture hitherto hidden from me.

After Jemmil and his friends had taken their leave I walked out into the desert courtyard of my new home in the Arab village of Mulladda and smelt the sweet fragrance of the desert night air. A dust cloud was moving across the heavens towards an otherwise full moon, the stars doing their best to shine through. I knew then that through Jemmil and his friends I was to see Oman under Arabian skies.

THE LAYWA

Jemmil was to become a regular visitor to my house as I was to his. We would also drive around from village to village.

It is interesting to point out that the pure-blooded Bedu is in fact quite white, apart from the jet black hair, eyebrows and lashes. It amused me once when Juma had been in the desert all day without his turban and when he returned he was complaining of the sunburn he had caught on his neck. If a Bedu goes to England for a six-month course in winter you will see his skin turns very pale. To the Arab we in the West are not regarded as white, but red or pink skin. If you go to Damascus in Syria you will really see white skin, sometimes like porcelain, with the dark features of hair and eyebrows and lashes.

After I had been living in the village of Mulladda for about six months and a frequent guest for dinner at Jemmil's house, where his wife would cook delicious foods, though the women would always eat separately from the men, Jemmil asked me if I would like to attend a traditional Omani dance. "Sure," I said, "I would love to. What is it called?"

"A 'laywa'," he replied. "Thursday evening, I will come and pick you up at your place at seven thirty."

At eight o'clock Jemmil arrived with his two buddies Saied and Salim grinning from ear to ear, punching each other playfully and generally acting like a couple of school kids. I got in the front with Jemmil. I was looking forward to this dance and had no idea what to expect or where it was to take place, yet was full of anticipation and excitement. We met up with a few other cars. There was the never ending exchange of greetings and oral rituals that Arabs go through when meeting friends or acquaintances, that one would think they had not seen each other for years, where in fact they had seen each other the day before in the market. Yet one had to suffer it gracefully and keep smiling all the way through, even when you had no idea what was being talked about. To show discomfort and impatience at this ritual would be the height of bad manners and would certainly not endear you to your hosts nor encourage them to invite you to their clandestine rituals. I felt, in a perverse way, that I was on my way to a secret Klu Klux Klan gathering in Mississippi in the 1960s, such were the various stages in the journey to where the dance would take place and the furtive air to the whole proceedings. Eventually we turned out to be part of a convoy winding our way through narrow desert tracks on this starless night, with a crescent moon hanging in the sky, as if it were dangling on a piece of thread like a mobile in a child's bedroom.

It was around 10.30 by the time that we arrived and there were at least one hundred cars gathered around a large clearing in the desert. The Omanis were largely divided into two groups. The older guys over twenty-five, who were all ceremoniously dressed up in Omani traditional gear, turban, long white dishdashas, belt with the dagger at the front and of course the ceremonial stick. The younger ones, perhaps in their teens, wore only the white dishdashas and the turbans which they had wrapped around lower parts of their faces so that only their eyes were visible. Incomprehensible comments were flying from the older men to the younger with a great deal of laughter in between. There was an air of flirtation in all these exchanges, the nuances of which I could not pick up. I just felt a specific tension/anticipation all around in that desert clearing. I dare not ask why as I felt that to do so would be to intrude on this other culture and although I had been invited it was as a spectator not a participant and I was determined to respect that and respect those who had invited me. I did not want to be like those appalling social anthropological journalists who have to be the centre of all things and ask the most inappropriate questions and appear to have no sensitivity to the culture in which they find themselves. I also think that those cultures whom they are trying to describe are somewhat put out by this deferential arrogance and actually feed these journalists misinformation or outright lies, which in many ways is poetic justice. I was quite happy to stand on the side lines and watch this spectacle as it began to take shape.

As we were walking towards the clearing I heard someone shout Jemmil's name and say something to him. I was quite sure his remark concerned me and asked Jemmil what had been said. Jemmil told me that this guy had told Jemmil not to tell me all their secrets. My intuition about remaining in the background had been correct.

Gradually a kind of hush descended on the previous gabbling and into the centre of the clearing one black Omani walked. He was carrying a musical instrument. It was some kind of horn. It was about a metre long, narrow at the front but gradually widened to a fluted end, which was quite wide. He raised the horn, put the piece to his mouth and blew a long single note that filled the desert air; it sounded like an African trumpet, yet its haunting quality was undeniable. It stilled the crowd who proceeded to encircle this piper. There were two circles, the first one composed of the younger Omanis who had hidden the lower part of their faces with their turbans. The outer circle was of the men with their sticks firmly planted on the ground. The notes changed subtly but surely and soon there was a rhythmic flavour to this evocative sound that permeated the whole desert. The boys on the inner circle would move slowly in one direction while the men on the outer section moved in the other direction. Slowly the tempo increased as did the pace of the dancing which was a slight movement of the body but definitely in keeping with the rhythm. This tempo soon became quite fast and the movement of all those present kept pace. There was a trance-like quality to the whole proceeding as if that were the intention of the piper to lead his dancers into a trance and eventually a frenzy. I found myself caught up in the whole thing. Swaying, my mind drifting, I felt outside myself, somewhere else, and I was only an onlooker. By now the trance state was leaving the dancers and the frenzy was taking over. The younger ones in the front were breaking the circle and running towards the piper where they would grab a handful of sand, turn to their friends, throw this in the air and let out some wild sound. Many of the younger ones did the same while the men on the outside moved around the circle with greater speed. Eventually the whole ritual reached a crescendo where the inner circle of boys collapsed as the men had dramatically increased the speed of their circular dancing. Then as quickly as it had begun it was all over. I looked at my watch and the dance from start to finish had taken over two hours. Yet it was less a dance and more a working up into a trance state where the spirit leaves the body and enters another different realm. What realm I have no idea and the purpose of this dance I never asked; probably it was to achieve this trance-like state: if so it was successful. We left after midnight quite drained and Jemmil took me home back to my house. I fell into a deep sleep as if I too had been sent into a kind of trance.

THE COMPANY OF STRANGERS

Juma and Abdullah returned from their voyage. Thoughts of Sinbad, swashbuckling sailors, scimitars, piracy, Jason and the Argonauts, the Golden Fleece, buried treasure and plunder on the high seas did cross my mind as I saw those two bearded pirate types disembark. I remember as a kid going to the Saturday morning cinema and my favourite films always had flying carpets, Sultans, caves full of jewels; without a doubt Sinbad was my favourite character and with him on his magic carpet I would fly off to distant lands.

And here I am in those distant lands. Juma and Abdullah had a few weeks' leave after their trip so returned to their respective villages. I was still settling nicely into my new house and everything was going well. Jemmil and his pals were still visiting and we were still going to Laywas and cruising around the villages, checking out what was going on. At weekends I would often drive to Juma's or Abdullah's village and spend the night there sleeping in the desert and in the morning bathing in the falaj. I had the best of both worlds. During the week we no longer slept in the desert, rather in my new house. Apart from enjoying the desert the main reason for sleeping outside was to get away from the Naval

Base. The new house had a wooden-beamed ceiling and being in the countryside attracted some welcome and other less than welcome visitors. Geckos were fine; they are like lizards and grow quite large and they are very useful in catching mosquitoes and flies. I certainly had an abundance of geckos. You could watch them on the rafters slowly stalking their prey and then in an instant their tongue would flick out and bye, bye mosquito.

Scorpions were some of the less welcome visitors and being largely nocturnal, one would catch them on the move at night. The best way to deal with a scorpion is to take off your sandal or shoe and whack so many times that it becomes pulverized. They are very fast and also blind, so that they react to sound only and if they think they have a chance the tail which contains the sting will rise up and they will attack you. This happened to me once. I was doing my weekly housework and on lifting the pillows I found a large black scorpion nestled under one of them. I shuddered at the thought that the night before my head had been resting on that pillow. So I froze for a moment, braced myself, and thought you are now living in the desert you will have to deal with these things yourself. So I reached for a Bedu stick and, feeling like Indiana Jones, flicked the scorpion onto the ground where I proceeded to attack it with my stick. I kept missing. The scorpion's tail rose and it charged towards me. I dealt what I thought would be a final fatal whack. My stick broke in two and the scorpion increased his pace running towards me. I was barefoot and ran out of the bedroom and slammed the door. So much for me emulating Harrison Ford. Having immediately forgotten my resolve at being independent, I rang Jemmil, thinking he would know what to do in a case like this. He was fast becoming my man Friday.

Within five minutes he was at the door. I led him to the room where the predator lay, no doubt anxiously waiting my return so he could sting me. I felt a little bit like the housekeeper in the film *The Exorcist* showing the priest where Linda Blair's room was, not daring to go in herself. I let Jemmil in and the closed the door, not wanting the scorpion to escape. Five minutes later Jemmil emerged with one dead scorpion, walked along the hall, slid open the bolt of the door to the desert courtyard, and threw out the dead scorpion only to find another, very live scorpion waiting on the doorstep with its tail up. It came in at great speed and with a vengeance; I wonder if it was the mate of the recently deceased scorpion and that they had communicated by telepathy. At any rate I sprang into action by running the length of the hall and climbing onto the fridge. Jemmil had left his sandals at the kill spot of scorpion number one, so was barefooted, the only weapon at hand being my broken stick. I urged Jemmil on, trying to encourage him, at which he started laughing. The scorpion was by now running around Jemmil's feet desperately trying to inject his poison, but Jemmil's nifty footwork, that would have put Michael Jackson to shame, avoided this all. He ran back into the room of scorpion number one, retrieved his slippers and dealt scorpion number two a final, stunning, deadly blow. I then climbed down from the fridge and opened my man Friday a cold drink, hoping he would not mention that in that scenario I was of no help to him at all. I knew he would be unaware of the saying "As useful as a chocolate teapot". He didn't say anything. However he did give me a telling look with those black eyes but I pretended not to notice and so I was able to recount my tale to my colleagues omitting the piece where I was standing on the fridge.

The scorpions were not to be my only unwelcome visitor. The camel spider was another such creature. If you wanted to mentally conjure up the most horrific, creepy, vile-looking living thing then you could do no better than come up with something that resembles the camel spider. It is called such because two or three of these creatures can bring down a camel. What they do is crawl to some fleshy part of the camel, inject it with a kind of anaesthetic, which makes the flesh go numb, and then feast on the meat of this camel. I heard one story, though I do not know if it is true or not, where someone in Aden, Yemen, woke up in the morning, after having been injected by a camel spider, and found he no longer possessed a bottom lip. The body of this creature is the size of a large ashtray that is to be found in pubs, its legs are nearly twice as long again. It is sandy-coloured and translucent so you can see red blood vessels running all through the inside of its body. It is incredibly quick. I was with Jemmil again, thank God, and we were watching a movie. Out of the corner of my eye I saw this, what looked like a piece of straw trying to work its way through a partially opened window. Then it came through. I jumped up, pointed it out to Jemmil, who grabbed his faithful all-purpose sandal and started chasing it around the house. It ran up the back of armchairs and all over the lounge with Jemmil in pursuit. I was giving Jemmil a running commentary as to its location, though it was hardly necessary. Eventually it ran into the kitchen area, which was very small. Jemmil followed it and I ran to the kitchen and slammed the door. I heard this whacking sound many times, then it stopped. I slowly opened the door and saw the camel spider dead on the kitchen floor, Jemmil standing over it. "Why did you close the door," he said.

"Well I didn't want it to escape and I knew that you had deliberately manoeuvred it into this space," I lied, "where there was no escape."

He gave me another one of those looks. I pretended not to notice again and went to the fridge to try and distract him with another cold drink.

Living in the country was fine in the winter time, but when summer time came the creatures from the plantations wanted somewhere shaded and they chose my house. On driving back home at night I would open the car door next to the door to the courtyard of my house. The interior light of the car would come on and as it did so I would see half a dozen scorpions running around. I opened the courtyard door and on entering I saw at least another half a dozen scorpions climbing the walls. The last straw was to be a spectacular and a unique occasion in the history of the arachnid species. Again I was watching a movie, this time it was with Juma. We had just finished eating, probably goat and rice, and large dinner plates were sat on the floor beside us. Very quickly Juma grabbed one of the plates and turned it upside down on something. "Why have you done that?" I asked.

"You are not going to believe this," he said.

"What?" I asked.

"Another spider. But this one is a little different."

"I do not believe you," I said. He slowly lifted one side of the plate and out reached a hairy black leg. I was later to learn it was what is known as a wolf spider and quite dangerous. Juma, who always had a devilish sense of humour, managed to manoeuvre this huge spider into a large fruit juice jug and cover the jug with the plate. Shall we give it a drink he says? Why not I reply I need one. So Juma removed slightly the large plate covering this grotesque thing and poured whisky inside. He covered the jug, whereupon after the spider had ingested this whisky, it jumped up and down several times and then fell stone dead at the bottom of the jug. I think that this particular spider must have been the only one of its species ever to die of alcohol poisoning. At least it died happily. I suppose for us it is the equivalent of drowning in a large barrel of beer. Juma was then going to shoot it as we had four rifles in the lounge. I told him I did not think it was necessary, it was already dead enough.

Juma and Abdullah were fond of their rifles and shooting things, so much so that we would target geckos on the rafters and see who could pop the most. It was quite interesting actually; a full-on hit, a bull's-eye, would bring the gecko straight down but as often as not a partial hit near the rear end and the gecko would just lose its tail, shed it and then go scurrying off.

I related all these tales to Jemmil, not the ones about gecko hunting but the creepy crawlies, and asked him his advice. I could no longer go on living with these things. He advised me to move as the situation would not improve and I think he was getting fed up with being my gamekeeper.

Jemmil found me a house immediately and quite close to his. So in fact there was no need to move back to the Navy, I would just move direct into my new home. During the move I was thinking to myself and then asked Jemmil aloud, "Am I the first white man to have lived in this village?"

"No," he replied. I must confess to feeling a little disappointed at this answer, seeing myself as some romantic hero, Thesiger-type figure, living in parts and cultures that were alien to most Westerners.

"So where was this other guy from?" I asked, thinking perhaps Scotland, Ireland or somewhere in Europe.

"Oh, he was from Egypt," Jemmil replied. Somehow I felt a little better after he had said that and could delude myself with this impression of me being an intrepid traveller. Then I thought of myself standing on the fridge while Jemmil battled barefooted with a scorpion. My delusions of grandeur were soon dispelled.

THE FORTNUM
AND MASON PICNIC HAMPER

In ancient Egypt cats were regarded as sacred animals and to a certain extent, although they were not regarded as sacred, they were certainly looked upon as useful in Oman. The same cannot be said of dogs who were regarded as dirty, the carrier of diseases, and people were not only wary of them but discouraged them from being in the village. On seeing a dog in the village young boys would hit it with sticks and throw stones at it driving it from the village into the desert where packs would form and roam at night. In packs the dogs had protection and were thus feared by the locals, alone they were vulnerable. So at night in the desert one would have to take care against these packs.

When I arrived in my new house Jemmil presented me a present of two cats – both female and both sisters. They proved very efficient at keeping rats, snakes and other unwelcome intruders at bay. They were feral cats but soon became domesticated and quite affectionate. They did seem to keep the nasties away and one time, just outside the front door, I found the remains of another wolf spider. They were also good in that they never brought their kill indoors. Except for one time. Juma had no time for the cats, and I am sure at times when I was not looking he would give them a kick. One night he came back late and was sitting in the lounge eating his supper. I was sleeping and when I awoke to the sound of someone retching. I got up and found Juma in the bathroom.

"What is the problem?" I asked.

"Look what your cats have brought to me." I went over to his seating place, where by now the cats had disappeared, and next to Juma's supper was a half-devoured large rat; maybe the cats thought it would be a nice entrée. They had obviously got their own back and when Juma was around the cats would not be seen and vice versa. They were sphinx-like in their looks and as pets behaved more like dogs. They would wait for me to come back from work. Each one would sit on opposite pillars of the entrance gate, transfixed, stone-like: they looked like statues. Unlike any other cats I know they would also love to travel in the car and would often jump in for a spin when I was going to the shops. I became quite attached to these two and when they became ill, I thought the obvious: rabies.

In the capital area, two hours' drive from where I lived was the surgery of the Royal Vet. This chap was an English doctor and he also treated the pets of English expats, the majority of which were dogs. I had decided to take one of my cats down to see him and check whether she had rabies or not. However I did not have a basket to transport her and as she was very weak I did not want her to roam around the car which would have made the trip hazardous. I enquired on the base as to whether anyone had a cat box; the answer was negative. However one very affected, but generous lady, said that she would loan me her "FORTNUM AND MASON" picnic hamper, stressing Fortnum and Mason three or four times, yet she said she would like it returned the following day as she and her hubby were going to a picnic and she was preparing the fare as we spoke: chicken breasts, pickles, cucumber and salmon sandwiches, a bottle of chardonnay was being chilled in the fridge etc. I duly thanked her and promised to return the precious hamper the following morning. I drove to my village, picked up one of the ailing cats, put her into the basket and drove to the vet. I was sat in the waiting room of the surgery with a variety of expats, mainly women, who were nursing pets varying from parrots, hamsters and cats to an enormous Great Dane. When my appointed time came I entered the consulting room with my cat and explained the problem to the vet. "Ah, we have a little problem," he said. "To find out if your cat has rabies we have to put her to sleep and then cut open her head and examine the brain."

"Well, doctor," I said, "that kind of defeats the object." He smiled and said it probably was cat flu and would give her an injection and he also forced a pill down her mouth, which she did not take kindly to. Yet he did say to me that I should watch out for foaming of the mouth from either cat as this would indicate rabies. He also informed me she was pregnant, which I thought was the last thing I needed, and with the look he gave me I felt the compulsion to say well I am not responsible for that, though I didn't. I duly thanked him, paid the bill and with the cat back in the Fortnum and Mason picnic hamper began my journey back to Mulladda.

I had gone about two thirds of the distance when I heard this awful howling coming from the basket. I drove on and turned up the music in the vain hope I would not hear her until I arrived home. Well this was not to be the case; the howling only got louder and eventually I had to pull over onto the hard shoulder. I slightly opened the lid of the hamper only to be greeted by a freaky sight. She was still howling but not only that she was foaming at the mouth very badly as if she had swallowed a box of detergent. I slammed the lid down, by now panicking and desperate to get home, but in my desperation and panic I had forgotten to secure the lid. I pulled over to the highway, accelerated to one hundred and twenty kilometres an hour when suddenly I heard this screech, the lid of the hamper flew open and on my left shoulder sat the cat from hell. She was foaming at the mouth and was dribbling down my neck. I drove over frantically to the inside lane and then to the hard shoulder where I opened the car door and ran out. I looked back in the car and she was still there foaming for Oman. I was faced with a dilemma that I had not experienced before. I was only twenty kilometres from home and thought if only I could get her back there and release her into the courtyard and let her run away there. I managed to tease her back into the foaming Fortnum and Mason picnic hamper. It also crossed my mind about the picnic tomorrow, but I thought a good scrub and mum's the word. All would be OK. With the basket safely secured I continued on the last leg of my journey.

After about ten kilometres there came this dreadful smell from the basket, I opened all the windows, to no avail, the smell persisted. I certainly was not going to open the basket again so I drove the last ten kilometres almost gagging. At last we arrived back in the villa. I closed the outside gates, dragged out the basket, flipped the lid open and ran away from the hamper. The cat's head appeared out of the top; she looked around, still foaming gloriously, found herself at home and ran off into the garden. I went to the basket to discover the source of the smell. It did not take long; the cat had had diarrhoea and the Fortnum and Mason hamper that was due to carry tomorrow's picnic was covered in muck and foam. I got a hose out and thoroughly washed it down and left it out to dry and air overnight. The following morning, rather sheepishly I returned the hamper, expressed my thanks and hurriedly drove off. I have often wondered...well never mind. The previous evening I had phoned the vet and told him about the foaming mouth. "Oh," he said, "do not worry the pill must have got trapped in her mouth and perhaps she may have suffered from a bout of diarrhoea too." Tell me about it, I thought.

The cats did recover quite quickly from their flu; however I was soon to discover that indeed both cats were pregnant and was at a loss as to what to do with the kittens when they arrived. Of course Juma's solution was to kill them all by some means I was not sure of. He obviously had something pretty evil in mind as he had still not forgotten their midnight gift. Personally I had no intention of handing them over to him when they did arrive. Oh well, I thought, I will cross that bridge when I come to it.

One afternoon I had some Omani friends visiting, one of whom was quite religious, so when prayer time came around, as it does five times a day, he asked if he could use my bedroom in which to pray. "Go ahead," I said. Now these cats were quite fond of this particular Omani and would follow him wherever he went. So as he left for the bedroom to pray they followed him into the room. After around fifteen minutes this chap came out grinning all over. "What are you laughing at?" I asked.

"Well," he said, "I am sure your cats are Muslims."

"Why do you say that?"

"Well as I was kneeling down to pray one cat sat either side of me and when I bent down with my nose to the ground in act of worship they followed me doing exactly the same thing." This caused a lot of laughter from all in the majlis.

And so the cats gave birth. As they were ill during their pregnancy several were deformed and consumed by their mothers, not a very pretty sight. I meantime was canvassing the base for takers of these kittens after they had been weaned and successfully managed to get takers for all but one. The future owners wanted to come and see and choose their particular kittens. However this was difficult as both cats, being feral, would hide their kittens daily, when I was out working. I found them in various places, in the wardrobe, on top of the wardrobe, under the bed and many other locations in the house. Eventually they were weaned and I had managed to farm out all but three. Of those three one was blind, but I was sure with a little help he would survive. Now the Commander of training had just arrived and his family was due out in a week's time. So he told me he would take two as his daughter was a real cat lover. The Commander himself was very short-sighted so I thought I would give him one able-bodied cat and the blind one also, in the hope that he would not immediately notice the blind one and as his daughter was a cat lover she may take pity on the weaker of the two. I drove to the base and to the delight of the daughter delivered the two cats. The following afternoon, while having a pint in the Officers' Mess, I was approached by the Commander who asked me if the cats were both alright. I asked him what he meant and he said that his family was playing with the cats with a piece of string and while one was chasing it around the other cat was just staring into space. "Well," I said, "they were both Ok when I delivered them to you."

The Bedouin of Sharkiya in the Wahiba sands.

Main path through Al Misfah (City of Stone).

Views from top of Jebel Akhdar (Green Mountain).

Hajar Mountain Range, Muscat Bay and Ornamental
Incense Burner.

Traditional Arab Sailing ship/Dhow Muscat Harbour

Omani stall holder, Muttrah Souq, Muscat.

Portugese Fort overlooking Muscat Plalace Harbour.

The tomb of the Prophet Job in Al Qarra Mountains, Dhofar

A Frankincense seller in Salalah, the capital of Dhofar.

Deserted house in the abandoned village of old Tanuf.

THE WEDDING

Abdullah and I were in the house in Mulladda when Juma burst through the door. He had a big smile. He said, "I have some good news." Abdullah and I waited in anticipation.

"Well come on, Juma."

"I am to be married in six weeks' time," he said. His courtship rituals had been successful and the decision was made; he was delighted. In Omani society a man is not considered complete and accepted as a full member of society until he is so married. Marriage customs are different in Oman and in many ways more egalitarian in so much as they draw up a contract to stipulate the terms of that marriage. A wife can insist on being the only wife, and if the husband breaks this agreement then punishment will be meted out on him; all kinds of various clauses can be inserted into this marriage so that each party will know the ground rules before they start. The Arabs, contrary to a lot of beliefs, do not buy their wives, they give what is a kind of dowry, and it can be gold, camels or a mix of many things. For Juma it was gold which cost him about ten thousand pounds sterling. This is in many ways a safeguard for the bride because if the husband does up and run away the wife will still have the gold that she could use to support herself and her family. The cost of a dowry does depend upon many factors and can be considerable. This is why many Arab love songs and love stories concern the pauper who has fallen in love with a rich man's daughter, the love is returned, yet the prospect of marriage is impossible because of the inability of the pauper to obtain the necessary dowry.

That night we had a party. A selected few were invited to my house. Towards the end of the party Juma suggested a shooting competition. My lounge was about forty feet long so there was ample space. We had several rifles at our disposal and the .22 calibre was chosen. I rigged up a target at one end of the room and we divided ourselves into teams. Well there were only two teams: myself and Jemmil, the Irish/Omani shooting team, and Juma and Abdullah, the Bedu shooting team. Shots did go astray but it was a very close-fought competition and not to say a bit anarchic. The Bedu, when shooting, will get down on one knee, aim then fire. I of course would stand and fire. Jemmil was not quite sure what to do and sometimes when he was holding the rifle I thought I saw a look in his eye that told me he would love to turn the rifle on the Bedu. Needless to say he behaved himself and fired at the target, not Juma or Abdullah. By now the target was shredded, the contest was officially called a draw and soon after everyone fell asleep. I awoke the following morning to the smell of cordite, bodies and rifles littered all over the floor. I went to check the "Target" and as I pulled it from the wall I was stupidly surprised by the fact that the wall was totally pitted with bullet marks. I remembered my landlord was coming to collect the rent the following day, so I managed to get hold of a poster and cover the offending wall. As it turned out the landlord did not even come in, he stayed at the door. However I sometimes ask myself what he thought when I left and he found bullet marks as he was preparing the house for the next tenant. Perhaps he scoured the garden looking for freshly turned earth expecting a bullet-ridden corpse to turn up there.

And so the wedding day approached. Juma was at home in Bani bu Hassan making the necessary preparation for the wedding. In the villages of Oman a wedding is a social event for all concerned. A few days prior, dancing and merry-making will take place in the village centre. It is one of the few occasions that the Bedu women have the chance to dance in public. The women will be dancing alone in separate rows opposite the men with a gap of about six feet separating them. It will be a rhythmic dancing with both sides edging forward and then retreating. The women would let out wails of jubilation using their tongues and making a distinctive howling cry, known as ululating; the men will remain silent. It was a tribal event in essence. Abdullah and I were to travel the night before and make our camp in the sands and take trips to and from the village. We saw Juma the night before the wedding and he took us around to show us the various preparations being made: the slaughter of goats, sheep and camels. The cooks were busy stirring large cauldrons containing the wedding meats. There was a slight reticence on the part of Juma when he was with us that I put down to nervous tension. However I was to find out it was the result of something else. Neither Abdullah nor I were a part of Juma's tribe and as such were not really welcome as total participants, rather as observers. Abdullah was aware of this and informed me so. I must admit I felt a great degree of disappointment as I believed the bond of friendship between myself and Juma was very strong. Consequently when the night of the wedding occurred we were left very much on the outside. I began to get restless and said to Abdullah, "Let's return back to our camping spot." Abdullah and I did return to our camping spot. Juma showed up about 4a.m. looking a little sheepish, talked a little with us and then returned to his new spouse.

The following morning Abdullah and I packed up and drove to his village to spend the rest of our time. His village was about a five hundred kilometre drive and on the way we passed magnificent scenery. Leaving the heat and glare of the red desert sands that skirted the villages of Bani bu Ali and Bani Bu Hassan, we drove north along roads that bore many signs saying "beware camel crossing" and we did see an abundance of camels. We then drove east and the landscape changed dramatically from desert, to scrubland and then to large mountains, presumably of volcanic origin, flanking us on both sides. These mountains were devoid of any real vegetation, just the occasional piece of greenery where you would see the goats scouring for food. The roads were almost empty and it was a magnificent drive with little roadside hamlets disappearing in a blink of an eye as we continued our journey to Ibri near Abdullah's home. We eventually arrived at Abdullah's village, just outside Ibri. We collected food from his house and drove out to gravelly-type desert that was a feature of Abdullah's particular region in Oman.

Subsequent to the wedding, and the reception, I did not see Juma for a few years. Both he and I knew the reasons why.

THE RETURN OF THE NATIVE

I have made my decision and know now that after what happened I can never return to the Navy or the Batinah coast again. Yet sometimes in my dreams I do return and see the old houses in which I lived, Jemmil and his friends and other people I knew sitting around laughing. I return to the Laywas and watch the assembled exotically dressed African/Omanis drawn into a trance by the lone piper, who conjures up the spirits of Africa long since forgotten in Africa but alive in the deserts of Oman.

I also return to the deserts where Juma and Abdullah and I had spent many evenings under the stars enjoying the essential essence of life, the desert skies and stars enveloping us like a huge blanket. I watch us as we drive across the mountains, wadis and through the deserts. I see us taking our bath in the falajes in the villages whilst feeling the tingling in my feet as the tiny fish clean my body. In many ways I am thankful for these vision-like dreams that have stayed with me since the exorcism and in other ways these dreams can be horrific, but given the choice I would not be without them; this is me now, I cannot change. Oman has entered in my blood and is coursing through my veins.

And so with my bags packed and in the back of a military pick-up I drove through the gates of the Navy and made my way back down the coast that I had driven up so many years before. Memories of that first day with Jassim come flooding back. I am quiet on my journey, looking out at the villages that I had got to know so well and passing the village where Jemmil and his family lived, past the stretch of desert which I had defiled with such disastrous consequences. The driver made several attempts at conversation but I was not very forthcoming. I had made many friends among the Omani officers in the Navy and among ordinary Omanis who worked outside the Navy. I had done so much, lived life to the full and learnt a great deal about myself. Now here I was leaving it all behind, onto pastures new, though at the time I did not think of them as pastures, rather as rocky grounds. Nonetheless it was my choice and I had to make the best of it.

After about one and a half hours we arrived at an Air Force base. The security guard checked my papers and we drove through to the Officers' Mess where I was to collect the key for my room that was to be my home, for a while anyhow. I felt the claustrophobia I had felt when living on the base of the Navy.

The driver helped me with my bags and we walked along the corridor to room B7. I turned the key of the door and entered, dropped my bags and lay on the bed and surveyed the room. It was a single room, sparsely furnished with a wardrobe, chest of drawers, a writing table, one armchair and two table chairs. There was a toilet and shower and all in all the room had the atmosphere of a sterile clinic. I drifted off to sleep for a few hours and awoke to the familiar sound of the Muezzin call to prayer. This was at about 6.30p.m. I got up, took a shower and decided to go to the Mess for something to eat. The restaurant was nearly empty: a few expats dotted around, sitting at different tables. There was none of the hum and buzz of conversation that I was used to. I ate my meal in silence and decided to go to the bar and have a drink and try and shake off this melancholy that had settled on me. I went to the bar and ordered a beer, then another and so on and reflected on my past life. I became merry; my gloom had lifted somewhat only as a result of quite a heavy alcohol intake.

I eventually left the bar, though not in a straight line, and made my way back to my room. Unfortunately all the corridors and rooms looked the same, which indeed they were. Eventually, after about half an hour, which when you are drunk could be anything from 10 minutes to one hour, I found B7 and thought to myself, this sounds like a prison number, and I felt like that too, living in this compound was living like a prisoner. It was then that I set my first priority of finding somewhere outside to live. "We pass this way but once…" I opened my door, took off my clothes, got into bed and for once, thankfully, fell into a deep, dreamless sleep.

The following morning I woke up, slightly the worse for wear. Nevertheless I remembered the previous evening and the promise that I had made to myself to find somewhere outside to live. It was a

Thursday so luckily I had no work, Thursday and Fridays being the weekends here. I left the room wearing a tee shirt, long shorts and a pair of sandals. In Muscat, having more expats and being more Western than the rest of Oman, one could get away with wearing shorts, not short shorts but ones that covered the knees; this was certainly not the case in the interior where long trousers or jeans were the order of the day. During the hot weather I really used to envy the Omanis in their long, loose dishdasha and sarongs, which they called wizaas, underneath, and sandals. They must have been so cool, but in jeans, shoes and socks, one became uncomfortably sticky. So Muscat had at least one advantage in that my outdoor wear was very cool. Muscat can get incredibly humid in the summer and it is not rare for temperatures to reach 45 Celsius.

I got into my Jeep and, having already decided that I would like to live by the ocean, drove in that direction looking for billboards that advertised flats for rent. Muscat is indeed beautiful, flowers on all the road edges, mosques of very elegant design. When I was there a Grand Mosque was being built by the Sultan; it is now a place where many people visit and it boasts the largest Persian carpet in the world. I returned to the base with several telephone numbers and made the appropriate calls. The real estate agents explained to me that as it was Thursday afternoon they could not arrange any viewing until Saturday afternoon. They arranged for me to view four different locations on Saturday after work. I felt content with my morning's work so went to the

Officers' Mess and had a bar snack and a few beers, thinking to myself life was not too bad and hopefully by this time next week I should be in an apartment of my own, by the sea, having a beer watching the fishing boats go by.

Saturday came and I met the real estate agent, an Indian expat. He showed me four flats; however after the first I knew there was no need to continue my search. The first flat was a one-bed roomed penthouse flat, with a huge lounge and patio doors that led onto a balcony that was in itself the size of the whole flat. It was facing due east and early in the morning, before the heat of the day had become too much, one was treated to magnificent ocean sunrises. From the balcony one could see the Indian Ocean and one had a direct view along the whole coast. Behind loomed the mighty Hajar Mountains that at sunset would change to a glorious red and pink colour; one could tell the time of day just by looking at the colour of the mountains. It was splendid. Here I was to make my home for a while and enjoy the facilities that Muscat had to offer that living in the interior did not.

MUSCAT

In 1970 Sultan Qaboos bin Saied Al Saied took the reins of control of Oman. He started what is known in Oman as the Omani Renaissance. In a country that was previously plagued by endemic disease, illiteracy and poverty, the Sultan established a modern government structure and launched a major development programme to upgrade educational and medical facilities, built a modern infrastructure and developed the country's natural resources. His success has been phenomenal and indeed Oman has undergone, in a very short space of time, a Renaissance under the auspices of Sultan Qaboos. He has created great loyalty among his armed forces and has chosen the highest ranking officers from all the different regions of Oman, thus creating cohesion and unity. His armed forces also act as a financial security net for the people of Oman in that they are the main employer and in large families the salaries of the young men contribute to the economy of the extended family culture which is so strong in Oman.

Muscat is now a modern city, though parts of it still retain its quaint antiquities. The actual town of Muscat is very small and many years ago at night, after sunset, two huge gates closed off the city to all outsiders, securing her for the night and protecting her against any intruders. These gates still exist, although renovated, and are functional. In the harbour inside the city walls sits the main Palace of the Sultan; the Sultan possesses many palaces throughout Oman. The palace setting is idyllic, just a small harbour surrounded by mountains.

On top of one of the mountains, just adjacent to the palace, is a spectacular fort built on a rocky outcrop. The fort's name is Al-Jalali and one can see it from the outside but there is no permission to enter. A soldier stands guard outside bearing arms and he will always pass the time of day with you, as most Omanis will. At night it is lit up and its sister fort on the corniche, the Al Mirani, is also illuminated and that makes it all look like a scene from a Disney movie.

Inscribed on the mountains of the harbour by the sailors are the names of ships that predate Napoleonic times. However Muscat harbour is far older than that. It belongs to the ancient classical world. It is not hard to imagine spices, silks, trading ships from the ancient world unloading and loading their cargoes in the port of Muscat. The port of Muscat was known to the ancient seafaring Greeks as "The Hidden Port", as it is difficult to find, couched in the Hajar Mountains. Old merchant tea houses are still to be found on the Muttrah corniche that sweeps its way gracefully along the harbour while the Mountains of Hajar hug that harbour as a mother would her child. These Hajar Mountains look unreal as if they had been made from papier-mâché but they are beautiful and make you feel the wonder and charm of Muscat and living in a land that time forgot.

On the corniche lies the old souq/market which existed during the classical age. Although it has been renovated it has been done in such a way that maintains its original atmosphere. One enters from the road through a small, narrow archway that widens slightly as you enter, where you find one major walkway that goes all the way through the souq. Off this walkway lie a number of narrower walkways that lead like a labyrinth throughout the whole of the souq. There is a riot of colours in the stalls that sell many fine fabrics laid out for all the passers-by; many of these stalls are staffed by Indians, others by Omanis.

There is an area that is devoted only to the selling of gold; gold is sold by weight, so many rials per gram. There are throngs of women decked from head to foot in black searching for gold trinkets while others are looking for complete gold dowries: necklaces, bracelets, earrings, anklets, all are to be found here. For the Omani the souq in Muscat is where they will come from all over the interior to buy their gold. Consequently you find a whole range of traditional costumes from all over Oman. Some women will be dressed head to foot in black, the faces of some covered by a black veil, the faces of others wearing a kind of leather mask worn by women from Saudi Arabia which is worn here by the women from Bidiya: a Bedu settlement that skirts the Wahiba Sands, not too far from the village where Juma comes from. Other women will show their faces just wearing a black scarf around their head. The men also will wear the costumes of their regions with turbans of different colours and worn in different ways; many will wear the small hat known as a kuma, as worn by Africans. The frankincense sellers are mainly from Salalah, the home of frankincense and the only place in Oman where you can find frankincense trees. These frankincense sellers are almost exclusively ladies, who sit squatting on the floor. Their bodies are usually of generous proportions; they are dressed in black but the faces are visible, ladies with pierced noses through which gold bands are threaded. They sell frankincense and myrrh; a small clay pot will be beside them where they will burn their exotic products advertising to likely customers their produce. If you want to buy gold or frankincense Muttrah souq, as it is known, is the best place.

This is the old part of Muscat and if you drive past the souq, towards the west, on your right you will see, perched on a rocky outcrop on a mountain plateau, a marvellous piece of modern Arab architecture: a giant incense burner that is also lit up at night. The drive will take you past the old town of Muscat and you will enter Sidab, a fishing village where people carry out their tasks in the time-honoured fashion. Fish are abundant here and fish is an essential part of the Omani diet. There is a wonderful fish market just east of the souq on the roundabout, where every fish you could think of you will find, including shark and every kind of shellfish. Drive past Sidab and you will come to a roundabout which indicates the end of the road. On the roundabout sits the original boat *The Sinbad* which was made in the traditional way and features in Tim Severin's *Sinbad Voyages* where he proved that boats such as these could sail to China and back. If you turn left at this roundabout you will follow a tree-lined avenue that will take you to the "Al Bustan", one of the most sumptuous and famous hotels in the world. It is built in traditional Arabic style and offers rooms adorned in Arab style or Western style. It is a marvellous place to stay. The staff are mostly Omani and dress in traditional costume. You can take tours to anywhere in Oman from here and one really feels that one is living in Arabia, but with the comfort of any first-class hotel in the West.

Turn right at the roundabout and left at the subsequent roundabout and you will climb a steep mountain on top of which is a viewpoint with a stunning vista of the hotel and nearby village and the sea. Continue along this road and eventually you will arrive at a small fishing village by the name of Qantab where few tourists visit and where those who have visited have left no visible mark on its traditional spirit.

The coastline of Muscat is absolutely magnificent, miles and miles of sandy beaches that are never crowded. The sea is warm and inviting and when one goes diving or snorkelling the coral is amazing. The clarity of the water is beyond belief and one can see a great deal of underwater life just by sitting on a boat. Off shore are rocky outcrops with naturally formed arches that allow you to sail your boat through; theses features are dotted all over the coast of Muscat and attract a great deal of sea life.

The whole area is like a scene from the film *Jason and the Argonauts*, anything more stunning is difficult to imagine. The coastline here winds in and out and you can follow these waterways and anchor anywhere and spend the day in marine bliss. Literally hundreds of deserted coves are to be found along this coastline, with small perfect beaches where you can spend the day in complete privacy. Indeed if a passing boat sees a cove occupied they will just pass by, wave and find a little cove of their own; they respect your privacy and expect you to reciprocate. It is strange how such a thing as being pleasant to one another makes the quality of life so much better.

In the marinas you can go dolphin watching as the seas around Oman are full of dolphins. Whales are also often spotted. There are sunset cruises around Muscat harbour on a traditional Arabian dhow. All along the harbour of Oman one will experience the magic of Sinbad and the ancient world of the Arab seafaring nation and a coastline and marine life that will take your breath away.

The remainder of Muscat is modern but is beautifully laid out and the buildings are designed in keeping with the Arab culture and immaculately maintained. There is plenty to do in Muscat as there is a wealth of museums, marinas, hotels. There are many five-star hotels that cater to the well-heeled Western traveller. The Omani tourist industry does not want to attract backpackers, so the hotels are first class and not cheap. Yet they offer all kinds of cuisines and facilities, health centres, swimming pools, and there are a virtual army of attendants. The roads are immaculately kept and one would not feel hesitant about hiring a vehicle and doing one's own thing. The roads in Oman are superb and full of four-wheel-drive cars, I think there are more four-wheel-drive cars per capita here than in any other country. The nature of the topography here make such vehicles essential so people can access their own villages that are often nestled somewhere high in the mountains where because of the elements, flash floods, rock falls etc. it is not possible to build black-top roads. Apart from Muttrah souq and that area there is no real town centre in Muscat, just a number of different centres and areas. It can be quite a distance between areas, for example from the Sahwa roundabout, which marks the beginning of Muscat, to Muttrah souq is forty kilometres. You will pass many shopping centres, Ghubrah, Al Qurm, a largely Western shopping area, Ruwi, largely sub-continentals, and many more.

One of the great saving graces of living in or holidaying in Oman is that it is safe. You have no fear for your personal safety and the Omani people are very gentle, friendly and helpful. If you are approached by an Omani it is 90% sure he is going to ask you if you need help. The Omani in the shop or the bank will always be courteous and you will never have to worry about being short changed or cheated in any fashion. However women should not travel alone and should dress in an unprovocative way, which means long-sleeve blouses and skirts. This is not so important in Muscat but absolutely essential when travelling outside Muscat. If one adheres to and respects the local ways one will receive a wonderful welcome and live an unforgettable experience.

This is Oman and these are the Omanis and their country is one where the spirit of Arab hospitality still exists and indeed thrives.

MIRIAM

I had by now spent two years in Muscat and was reasonably content. There are so many places to visit, deserts, mountains ruined cities, ancient sites, bronze-aged settlements dating back to 3000 BC which all verified that Oman was a key player in trade with the ancient world. There is a wealth of historical treasure to be found in Oman and there are many pieces of the historical jigsaw puzzle that remain missing and which people are continuing to look for. Even further back than the classical age there is evidence of early man living in Oman as revealed by the many cave paintings which are to be found in Dhofar and the North of Oman.

However living on the coast of Oman provided me with a unique opportunity to view life under the waves. Oman is said to be the most unspoilt diving and snorkelling area in the world and because Oman has just opened her doors to the tourist, the underwater world is still intact. Not being a strong swimmer, I used a Jet Ski life jacket and went snorkelling for the first time in my life and discovered a beautiful world that hitherto had been unknown to me. The coral and fish life were like a kaleidoscope of natural beauty. I saw sharks, which were shy and just swam off, giant turtles that look so comical and sometimes ungainly when they swim on the surface and so many different coloured coral fish and in such great numbers that sometimes it was like swimming through a cloud of colour. Only after watching David Attenborough's *Blue Planet* did I come anywhere near seeing such beauty as I had seen under the waters of Oman.

I mostly kept myself to myself and would drive long distances, take many photographs and generally soak up all that Oman had to offer. Then, one afternoon I received a phone call. It was a voice that I had not heard for more than four years; however it was a voice that I would recognize till the end of my days and that would haunt me in my dreams. "Hello, Rory, this is Juma, how are you?"

"Fine, Juma," I replied, "and you and the family. Where are you?" I asked.

"In Muscat," he said, "with my family and I now have a little daughter whom I want to show you." Now unless you are Omani and or Muslim it is unlikely that you will be invited to meet Bedu women. Of course I was very flattered and said I would love to see him and his new daughter. One cannot say in Arab society that I would love to meet your wife; this is absolutely forbidden as it implies you are desirous of his wife. Nonetheless I was keen to meet her. I gave Juma my address and half an hour passed and the door bell went. There was Juma, same as ever, broad grin, beaming smiles with a strikingly handsome Bedu face. He was in traditional dress, with his turban, kanja, the curved silver dagger and belt and his Bedu stick. His wife was covered from head to toe with a long black veil making her visual features impossible to discern. In her arms she carried Miriam bint Juma. Miriam the daughter of Juma.

"Come in, you are welcome." They all came into my lounge which was decorated in Omani style and all the seating was on the floor. As everyone sat I brought in soft drinks, a platter of fruit and some pistachios from which everyone helped themselves to all. Fatima, Juma's wife, took off her veil and acted quite naturally. Juma said this was Ok as he considered me like one of his brothers, a part of his family; I was flattered, honoured and humbled. There is a wonderful trait in the Omani, that I learnt when I had had disagreements with Juma and Abdullah, what has happened in the past is finished, over with, not to be referred to again, forgotten; it is the now that matters, not even the future for that lies in God's hands. As John Lennon said: "The future is what is happening to us now."

Miriam was wearing a tiny gold chain with an equally tiny gold locket containing a miniature Koran; she was shy, burying her head in her mother's lap. I was asked to hold her; it was then, as she wriggled in my arms, that I sensed something was not quite right. I looked into her eyes and then into the eyes of her mother and father, Juma smiled. "Yes, Rory, she is brain damaged; Fatima had a caesarean operation and our little Miriam was damaged during her birth, but Al-Hamdillilah (thank God) she did not die, and she is with us now and we love her very much. She has brought us great happiness."

I was speechless, one of those rare occasions when I did not know what to say, however the words came and as I returned her to her mother I said, "Juma, she is beautiful." Juma told me how they were expecting another baby, his wife blushed as Juma pointed to her stomach. He told me he was very happy and that he had now found the woman with whom he was to spend the rest of his life, the woman he was to grow old with, and they would have more children, lots of grandchildren who would eventually look after him and Fatima when they were old in their lovely village on the edge of the desert. I felt a kind of sadness about my own life which had none of what Juma mentioned and thought how wonderful life would be if it were so simple and harmonious. I must have been quiet and reflective for Juma said, "Why are you so quiet, Rory?"

"Just thinking," I replied.

After staying for about an hour Juma said they must travel home as they wished to arrive back in their village, three hours' drive from Muscat, while it was still light. I saw them to their car, an old Toyota, waved them good bye, a happy family unit, laughing with each other as they were driving away, totally interdependent, accepting of all and thankful for what they had. Fate had dealt them with what may have been a harsh blow in the West, but here it was the will of God and who can go against His will.

THE GUN SOUQ/MARKET.

"Allah Al Akhbar Allah," God is great. It is 5.40 a.m. and the faithful are called to the first of the five daily sessions of prayer that is one of the duties of the Muslims and quite a few are off to the mosque. The mosque itself is new and the size of a moderate church in England. It does not have a spire, rather a tall tower of brilliant white (a minaret) on which rests a small green globe. Much further down on top of the first floor is a much larger dome, also green but with intricate Arabic design in gold that runs in lines to meet together at the summit of this dome. In a rather perverse way this has become my early morning alarm clock. As my apartment is situated very close to the mosque it is very difficult to sleep through the timeless resonance of that chant from the muezzin, as in the minaret on top of the mosque are usually speakers which amplify this call. However this is convenient for me as it marks the beginning of the day and another sunrise in Oman and it is at this time of day that the weather is at its coolest and frequently a gentle breeze is blowing from the Indian Ocean. It is an exhilarating time of day and makes one feel alive and glad to be so.

I am off on a trip that will take me into the interior of Oman. Oman has previously been two countries, Oman and Muscat. The interior before had been governed by a succession of religious leaders known as the Imam, his seat of power the capital town of the interior, Nizwa. Nizwa is about one hundred and forty kilometres from Muscat although how much control the Imam had of his peoples in this vast area is somewhat doubtful. The interior was made up of a multitude of tribes who to all intents and purposes seemed to possess a large degree of autonomy; the only characteristic linking them was their adherence to the one faith, Islam, that of the Ibadhi sect, not of the majority Sunni sect nor its second largest sect the Shii'a.

I have many villages and towns to visit on my journey through the interior so an early start is essential. I leave my apartment at 6a.m. and get into my Jeep, drive past the mosque, outside of which is a vast quantity of sandals as the faithful have to enter the mosque barefooted. I turn left past the mosque and drive south. In the rear view mirror I see that the sun has moved over the Hajar Mountains and is three quarters full casting a wonderful clarity of light over these mountains, yet the brightness of the sun causes me to flip the rear view mirror into night mode. There is no need, as yet, for air conditioning in the car so I wind down the windows and enjoy the cool air blowing around my body. I arrive at the airport roundabout and am reminded at this point that until the 1970s this is where the tarmac road stopped and from here on it was all dusty tracks, marked with the telltale signs of camel caravan trains who brought their agricultural goods to Muscat to sell and returned equally loaded with the produce that they needed to sustain themselves in their respective villages. These journeys would take days. Fortunately now there is tarmac road all the way to Nizwa and beyond, and this programme of building black-top roads is still underway and there remains a great deal of work still to do. Only recently have many villages in the interior had electricity connected and it was with great joy and pride that my students used to come to class announcing proudly to all that their village now had electricity. Still many remote areas are without electricity and work off generators. The topography of the country makes so many villages inaccessible and thus incredibly difficult to connect to the main grid. Also the elements that unpredictably bring with them flash floods have washed away electric lines, and new roads that had only been constructed a few weeks previously, become impassable. Large boulders that have been displaced by the force of the water block many mountain passes and roads so that on one day a perfectly clear, drivable tarmac-covered road has been transformed into boulder-strewn track, passable only by climbing over the litter of debris from the flood of the day before.

And so I drive past the airport on a brand-new three lane highway that is literally empty. Here in Oman the pleasure of going for a drive or spin still exists as the weather is always fine; there are many beautiful vistas and most important of all the traffic is very light. My first destination is to the market town of Fanja, some forty kilometres outside of Muscat, yet I have come to visit one particular part of this market, or souq as it is called in Arabic: that is the area where they sell small- to high-calibre rifles. Fanja marks the end of Muscat territory and the beginning of the region known as Dakhliyah. It seems amazing to me and almost beyond belief that you can go and buy a rifle and ammunition without even showing any form of identity and walk away and carry these arms quite legally.

In the near distance I see, perched on a hill, an old sandstone- and mud-built fortress, dominating the skyline and all the surrounding area. I head towards this fortress through a labyrinth of extremely narrow and twisting roads. At the side of these run the falaj which irrigate all the date trees growing in this area. It is sometimes difficult not to drive straight off the road and into these plantations but with forbearance I manage to arrive at the entrance to the fort without any serious mishap. The entrance to the fort is a narrow archway and standing in the middle is a splendidly attired old Omani; a long white beard flows down his brilliant white laundered dishdasha, the two whites blending together.

I dutifully acknowledge him in Arabic, "Salaam Alaekum," and he returns my greeting with a broad grin, igniting a wonderful sparkle in his eyes, "Alaekum Salaam." He shakes me by the hand and obviously because I have greeted him in Arabic he believes I am fluent, which is very far from reality. He then beckons me to follow him me, talking incessantly, while I grin and laugh and make expressions of incredulity at what I think are the appropriate times. He proceeds to show me proudly around the fort, which is largely dilapidated, small staircases only half intact, walls fallen down, but we tramp quite merrily through the fort both absorbed in a conversation that neither one of us understands, yet that was not important; the importance was that there was some kind of communication, not only oral but spiritual. Someone said that language was a very primitive form of communication; how right he was. It is important in Islam that all people of the faith are treated as brothers and therefore they are expected to be nice to one another, not told what to do, rather asked in a polite way if they would possibly mind doing something. This is the way of the Omani and it is a way that suits my way of thinking too. When the tour is finished I offer my profuse thanks in Arabic, which takes ten times longer than it does in English. The Omani governed by strict rules of protocol in turn tells me I am welcome, which again takes ten times longer. While this is happening I am thinking to myself, I wonder if he would mind if I took his photograph. I would dearly love a black and white picture of this real gentleman on my wall at home. He assents willingly and poses for more than one shot; he even in jest lifts a little of the hem of his dishdasha, showing a bit of ankle. I laugh with him. As I am writing this I am looking at that fine old man whose picture is hanging in my lounge.

I drive back through the labyrinth and down into the souq where there are by now a vast quantity of people milling around buying foodstuffs and clay pots, the parking of the cars in a haphazard way, any place one can find and most of the people are driving pickups, either red or white pickups. These are the two most predominant colours and you rarely find a pickup of another colour, or perhaps they just make them in red and white, a bit like Henry Ford who said of his Model T car, "You can have any colour as long as it is black." These are an agrarian/pastoral people who buy and sell their produce at the nearest market, and for them the nearest market is Fanja. This is their area and this is where they belong in the great cosmos of life. Meanwhile I stroll around the souq, looking and feeling very suspicious, I cannot bring myself to ask someone where the place where I can buy a rifle is.

Furtively I stick my head into shop doorways, for though most of the market is outside I could not for the life of me see any rifles on display. Then I hit the jackpot. In one small, dusty old shop, like a Dickensian bookshop complete with dust, I find what I have been looking for, the Gun Shop. All around me are rifles of varying ages, some brand new, others relics of a bygone age; some even looked like muskets, but I was told the new ones were from Czechoslovakia. I browsed, feigning a little knowledge, of which I had none, picked up a few rifles and looked down their sights, asked prices and if they had ammunition for the rifles, to which they answered they had all I needed. At that point I realized I had no idea what I would buy or if I really wanted one, but most important of all would I, or rather someone else, be safe if I possessed a lethal weapon. I then thought that the world and I would probably be a safer place if I did not possess a weapon of this nature. I said my goodbyes and got into my Jeep and headed for Nizwa knowing that I had made the right decision.

THE ROAD TO NIZWA

On leaving Fanja I cross a huge bridge with an equally huge wadi, a dry river bed that during one of Oman's flash floods becomes a raging torrent. Huge articulated trucks have been taken by these swirling waters and more than a few lives have been lost. There are many wadis in Oman and many times these wadis are named after particular tribes and mark the boundary of the territory of these tribes. In times gone by it was when one tribe would cross into the territory of another that the fighting would begin and once one life was lost a vendetta that could last for centuries would continue between tribes. This is now largely extinct; however the practice of honouring one's tribe and marrying within it is still very strong.

In almost every household outside Muscat there is at least one rifle. These are carried openly. In the desert the Bedu have their territory finely marked and certain wells and grazing areas will belong to one tribe while others to another. It was only usually in time of drought when one tribe's livestock overstep tribal boundaries and graze on the territory or use a well of another tribe that conflict and violence really could occur. I am reminded of that iconic opening shot in David Lean's film *Lawrence of Arabia* where, in the distance, one sees a camel, ridden by Omar

Sharif, approaching a well that belongs to his tribe but that is being used by another. Omar Shariff proceeds to shoot the interloper.

Driving on towards Nizwa one sees, perched on top of small hills or mountains, old lookout posts, built like mini forts, where tribesmen would maintain watch over their villages and crops lest someone from another tribe would come and pilfer or even worse raid their village.

The area on the road to Nizwa is incredibly fertile and the roads are lined with date trees and other crops and old sand and mud watch towers and forts and lush green palms. Passing through these villages one really has a sense of being in the Arabia that one has dreamt about. Further back, on the right side of the road, are incredibly high mountains and escarpments. It is here that when the rains come they travel down these mountains and flood this fertile plain. There is nothing more terrifying than being caught in one of these flash floods. It happened to me once on this stretch of road to Nizwa, and I had to remain in my car the right side of the wadi and watch as cars and trees were swept away by the immense force of this flowing river. You cannot turn back as there will be another wadi a few miles on in the same raging state. So you are left in between and you just have to sit it out desperately in the hope that the wadi does not overflow and engulf you in its anger.

On the road to Nizwa one passes Jebel Akdhar (the Green Mountain). It is the second highest mountain in Oman, after Jebel Shams (the Mountain of the Sun) and rises to nearly ten thousand feet. This has only recently been opened to civilians without a pass, but they must have a four-wheel-drive as the mountain is so steep a normal saloon car would not be able to cope. It is not called the Green Mountain for nothing. The climate here is much cooler than the rest of Oman and here are grown grapes, pomegranates, cherries and all sorts of wonderful fruits. Many people visit this mountain when the heat is unbearable in Muscat and now a hotel has been built on top to accommodate the Western traveller.

Jebel Akdhar is very mountainous and steep, and before the road was built almost inaccessible to the outsider. Sheer cliff faces are all around and paths, known only to the mountain dwellers, are the only way up to the summit. These passes are no more than donkey trails, but if you did not know where they were then you were stuck. It is said that the Persians, when in Oman, did manage to assail this mountain and when they arrived at the top and found its climate to their liking and the people so friendly they decided to stay and intermarry. Today it is not unusual to find Arabs from Jebel Akdhar with green eyes, a legacy no doubt of the Persian settlers. It is certainly true that on the other side of this mountain, where the Batinah coast is and the town of Barka at which the Persian occupiers were defeated and expelled by the Omanis, Persian tribes decided to stay in this magnificent country. There is a large tribe called the Al-Farsi in these parts, some of whom have migrated to Muscat. Farsi is the language spoken by the Persians/Iranians so any of the Persian settlers were given the tribal name of Al-Farsi (the Persian one) by the tribes of

Oman. Indeed as the Persians are Shii'a Muslims one does find Shii'a mosques in Oman, plus a Catholic cathedral and Protestant churches. The Sultan, admirably so, is very keen on freedom of religious expression.

I arrive at a roundabout at the end of this long road of spectacular scenery. Turn left – Salalah, the province of Dhofar, the "garden of Oman" nine hundred kilometres away. The road does not much look like a garden as there are over eight hundred kilometres of desert to cross before you come to the Mountains of Dhofar. Turn right and it is ten kilometres to our destination, the base of power of the Imam religious ruler of Oman for so many centuries.

The approach to Nizwa is stunning: the skyline is dominated by the huge gold and blue dome and the tall tiered minaret next to it on which sits another smaller blue and golden dome. This mosque has recently been renovated and around it a new souq has been built and this area contains the very heart of Nizwa. With this vista in front it is hard not to be in awe, yet also on your left hand side runs a wadi, which, though not as large as that of Fanja, can turn into a raging torrent during the rains. I approach a smaller roundabout and drive straight on and turn left into a vast car park that has been built with the new souq and mosque. I park my Jeep between two pick-ups, a red one and a white one, strange that, and make my way to the entrance of the souq. In the car park are some larger gated lorries that are full of cattle. Cattle are only to be found in Dhofar, so these calves and cattle have made a long journey to be here. But then I realize the holy festival of Eid, which celebrates the end of Ramadan, is approaching, and it is Muslim tradition to feast well at this time so there is going to be a lot of slaughtering going on. This slaughtering can take place in your garden or commonly at the falaj where the running water takes the blood away. Literally speaking, at Eid the falajes are running with blood from the goats, sheep, cows, and camels that have been slaughtered in the time-honoured fashion, that the Koran dictates. That is the throat of the animal must be slit and the animal is to be turned upside down so the blood can flow out of the carcass. This meat is called Halal and all Muslims and Jews are forbidden to eat the meat of an animal that has not been slaughtered in this way.

The entrance to this modern souq, which has been built in traditional Arabic style, is a beautiful stone archway with two immense wooden doors, one on either side. On passing through this entrance one feels as though one is going back in time; all the Omanis are dressed superbly in their traditional dishdasha, holding sticks, and wearing the curved silver dagger in sheaths attached to belts. This area is very traditional and conservative and as is common in all Oman when people go out publicly, they make sure they are dressed correctly, so when out shopping the Omanis, even young kids, are impeccably turned out. In the West we tend to dress down; if you dress down out here it is something that is frowned upon.

I thought I was in heaven as the first two shops I entered were stacked full of rifles on the wall, along with kanjas, ammunition boxes in glass cases, along with traditional handmade Omani silver artefacts. Some were antique, like the anklets; however attractive they were they looked a little sinister as they resembled shackles. There were thick, heavy silver bracelets and ornate necklaces all in silver. The Souq of Nizwa is a wonderful place to visit to buy Omani souvenirs; there are the traditional walking sticks and clay pots, a whole array of goods that makes it so difficult to choose from. Unlike the Muttrah souq in Muscat, in Nizwa all the shopkeepers and servers are Omani and they are so graceful and polite and are not into hard selling and beam smiles at you whether you buy or not. Just adjacent to this block of shops is the fruit and vegetable souq, also new, and a walk through this and you enter a warehouse full of fresh exotic and familiar foodstuffs. Here one is in the hub of Omani life, no longer an outsider, tourist or voyeur. If you arrive early enough between seven and eight you pass through the veg souq which will bring you out to the livestock souq. Here the sellers will walk their livestock around a small dusty perimeter while the assembled circle will shout their bid for the animal being displayed. All in all it is a great day out. Nizwa fortress, the political seat of the Imam, is just adjacent to the souq and a visit here gives one a feel for the history of Nizwa and the important part it has played in the history of Oman.

The deserted village of Tanuf lies ahead of me. The village of Al-Misfah, carved out of stone from the mountains more than two millennia ago, beckons me to her, as does the pre-Islamic fort and the sorcerers of Bahla sat around the ancient tree in the village square. The potters are at work moulding their vessels from the kilns that they have been using since the dawn of time. Jabrine, the seventeenth-century fort, was the seat of scholarly pursuits in Oman and produced some notable figures. The ancient beehive tombs that belong to the Bronze Age, five thousand years ago when Oman was known as Majan, sit majestically on a hill top. Beyond that lies Dara, a desolate area, peopled by Bedu who traverse this desert gravelly terrain and after that a mountain range that will take me from the interior back to the Arabian Sea. But for now I am tired. I check in at a hotel in Nizwa, stand under a cold shower, change and walk into the local bar where I allow several cold lagers to wash away the dust that I have acquired on my journey through time, history and tales of Arabia.

THE VILLAGE OF THE ACCURSED.

As I leave Nizwa early the following morning, the sun just peeking over the blue dome of the magnificent mosque, the crenels of Nizwa fort being penetrated by the sun's rays, the town is already a bustle: people are going about their business; the pickup drivers are arriving in the new car park with their fresh fruit and vegetable produce ready for a day's work. The shopkeepers are unfastening the bolts that locked the shutters the night before, sliding these shutters up, announcing to the world another day had begun and the traders were open for business.

An Indian worker yawns and rubs the sleep away from his eyes as I approach the roundabout that exits Nizwa. Now here on this roundabout is a pile of concrete books, giving credence to the belief that really you can put anything on a roundabout. This reminds me of one occasion when someone with an over developed sense of creativity placed an artificial horse right next to the roundabout at Barka. However at night the horse looked very realistic and drivers believed the horse was running straight at them and, swerving to avoid this horse, many cars ended up on the roundabout. The horse was removed six months later after more than a few drivers had experienced the runaway horse of Barka.

I am bound for the deserted village of Tanuf.

The road from Nizwa to Tanuf climbs a little and then drops into a straight, even road, a wide plain, farmsteads on either side, a semi-arid region that no doubt has plantations not visible from the road. Ten kilometres from Nizwa I see a sign that says Tanuf right, eight kilometres. As I drive down towards this village the black-top suddenly ends and I am once more on a sand track. I can see little towers of sandstone and mud and as I get closer a whole town makes itself visible to me. I get out of the car. It is even now quite hot, the sky a cloudless blue; there is great stillness in the air and a dragonfly hovers close by and then darts across my path. The village is absolutely deserted and houses are in half ruins. No one is around: usually in deserted villages you will see someone moving around but here there is a very tangible menace that accentuated the emptiness of the village.

A sand lizard scurries across the sand next to my boot as I enter a dilapidated building. A small eddy of wind whips through the town and, as I turn my face away from it, I see a building in which there are alcoves and inside the alcoves the pages of a book are being turned by the wind. I feel my flesh crawl and believe that the jinn have once again crossed my path, yet I am determined not to cross theirs. I enter the building to look at this book that has been there for nearly fifty years. I find myself in the old mosque of Tanuf and the book whose pages are being turned is a very old copy of the Koran. I look for a shaded place and sit down to drink some water.

Tanuf lies at the foot of the Western Hajar Mountains that loom large above it. As I raise the bottle to my lips I gaze up to an escarpment where I see a lone figure staring down at me; he appears to be from a different time, another era. There is a poignancy here that I cannot quite grasp; it is as if he has some message to give me from the past. We are men from two different times yet at that moment in time our spaces have crossed. The sun is in my eyes and I cannot make him out clearly. I move to a different position to get a clear view but by this time the figure has disappeared and any message he had for me is lost forever. I move back to my shaded spot wondering if the figure had been real or just a trick played by the light.

After being quiet and still for a while I stare down to the falaj which, although it still has water, that water is dirty and stagnant through lack of maintenance over the last forty years. Flies, dragonflies and all sorts of insects are to be found. I leave the mosque and walk into the now empty dwellings and try to picture life as it had been here so many years ago when the village was alive. I see families gathered around large platters of food eating and talking together, children running and playing in the dusty roads and some of the more adventurous ones trying to climb the mountains that dominate Tanuf. There is a great sadness about the town. For how long has this settlement, existed, perhaps thousands of years, and been a home to all those generations of people who went before and whose spirits lingered on in the still, hot desert air. Who really knows what catastrophe led to this village being abandoned. On leaving the village I feel the presence, almost hemming me in, of the ghosts of those people who forty years earlier left their sanctuary and knew that they could never return and that the life they had known was lost and gone forever.

THE CITY OF STONE

I left Tanuf feeling depressed and oppressed. It was a town of great melancholy and not a happy place at all. I was happy to leave her behind me. I arrived at the junction of the main road and took a right onto the highway. I put a cassette in the player and relaxed into the seat of the car and took the road that would lead me to the "City of Stone". The Eagles were playing Hotel California, "On a dark desert highway…" so I just tuned into the music, relaxed and let the landscape fly by. Some fifteen minutes after Tanuf I had to take a right turn at a Shell petrol station. When asking directions from Omanis, petrol stations are the most common marker. The road was to take me to Al-Hambra, from where I was to engage four-wheel-drive and ascend the mountain in order to reach my destination. The Eagles were still playing as I drove along – "I get a peaceful easy feeling…" and the blues that had possessed me in Tanuf were quickly disappearing. I was by now looking forward to my next stop on this overland voyage.

Just before we arrive at Al-Hambra there is a sign that says "Wadi Ghul turn left" and it is from here that one climbs into the "Mountain of the Sun", Jebel Shams, and the highest mountain in Oman. I drive past here and enter Al-Hambra and drive through the town centre, and at a small roundabout turn right. This leads me across a forded falaj and to the foot of the mountain that will take me to Al-Misfah. I engage my car in four-wheel-low and begin a rather rough drive that shakes my car, my body and unfortunately The Eagles, whom I remove from the player. The road is dusty and the car goes down steep declines and up rough inclines; some vehicles pass by the other way and it is important to keep one's concentration. Yet the higher you rise the more spectacular the scenery below appears. One sees the Mountain of the Sun rise towards its namesake and left of that is a massive plain that serves for subsistence farmers with huge earth-coloured rocks that look as though they have been scattered here and there by some giant from Megalithic times.

On and on I climb. The road becomes steeper and narrower and as I cross the brow of a particularly narrow, steep piece of road I get my first glimpse of the city made from stone: Al Misfah. It is quite a stunning sight. There is a large, craggy rock on top of which sits a house. From where I am I cannot see how one could enter this house as the front was a sheer rock face. There must be some entrance around the back, and of course there was. In front of me stood the city but the only entrance looked like the entrance to a cave. It was high enough and wide enough only for one adult at a time to pass through. Through the opening one could see nothing, just blackness. Outside the entrance was a small coffee-type shop where half a dozen old men were sat on a bench. These were wiry mountain men, short in stature and lean: one could imagine that their bodies had been adapted to the terrain where a lot of mountain walking was necessary. They all had long white beards, white turbans, they carried sticks and all of them wore the traditional kanja.

I left my car and walked towards them. "Salaam Alakeum," I cried to which in unison they gave the universal Muslim response of, "Alakeum Salaam." They all stood up and I shook their hands in turn. We engaged in the standard protocol of never ending greetings, of asking them how everything was to which they would all reply, "Al-Hamdillilah." Then I asked them for permission to look around their village. Welcome they replied. I had heard about the beauty of Al-Misfah before but nothing could prepare for the delight and awe which I encountered when I walked through the cave-like entrance. It was a city or town that indeed had been carved out of stone, like the monasteries in Ethiopia. The pathway was narrow, and either side were entrances that wend their way around into dwellings. You could see no doors, just cave-like openings that would vanish into darkness. A woman dressed all in black hurried past me and scurried through one of these black openings. The buildings were tall and it was only at about twenty feet up that one saw small openings that were to act as windows. I suppose that in the excessive heat of summer these stone dwellings must have been extremely cool and in the winter easy to keep warm. The pathway headed down so I followed it until the end, where there was a large tank-like reservoir carved out of the mountain that served to irrigate and also for the youngsters to swim in. At the foot of this stone tank the land slid down onto cultivated terraces where lemon trees and other trees grew; the falaj ran along the top of these terraces and every so often was diverted to water some other crop. The view down the mountainside was awesome and green, so incredibly fertile and lush. There was the shade afforded by the lemon trees that I sat under which diffused the rays of sunlight and the smell from the citrus was intoxicating to the point that I fell asleep for an hour.

When I awoke it was as if in a dream. I must have been in a deep sleep for at first I had no idea where I was. Then I remembered and looked across at the mountain range facing the mountains that I was on. On a ridge were six or seven conical stone-like constructions, of about eight feet tall and at the bottom about six feet wide. I had heard of these and there was very little known about the purpose of those who built them. They were referred to as beehive tombs and were dated to the third millennium BC, five thousand years old. Who had built them and why, and what kind of civilization did these people live under? Were they the graves of local heads of tribes, did they serve some ancient religious practice? The strange thing is that in Europe such structures exist. What was the link five thousand years ago between places like Ireland and Oman? Was there a link? These were the questions that I wanted answers to. These beehive tombs were a very prominent part of the landscape and anyone living there at the time would see them every day. They stood majestically on the mountain ridge like sphinxes from ancient Egypt. They must have been of great significance, but for what I do not know. The most famous of these beehive tombs are situated in a small town near Bat and they are placed on a ridge and can be viewed for many miles around. Behind them lies a white mountain known as Jebel Mischt which serves to highlight these tombs. Was that why they were built in that location? No one so far has come up with any explanation at all.

And so I climbed onto the path that led out of the village. It was late afternoon and the people were beginning to stir after their afternoon sleep. The whole city could have been a set from *Indiana Jones and the Temple of Doom*, but there was no feeling of doom here, just peace, tranquillity and a sense of timelessness. I have no idea how old Al-Misfah is, neither did anyone I asked, but the feeling was that of belonging to an ancient time, a classical age. I exited through the cave-like entrance and turned back. You would never think that beyond that blackness, to my mind, lay one of the great wonders of the world and I felt privileged to have seen it and thankful to the old men who had given me their permission to do so.

MAGICIANS AND SCHOLARS

I drive away from Al-Misfah with a sense of awe, yet also a sense of loneliness. I miss not having shared that experience with someone and I think back to the not so distant past where if circumstances had been different Juma and Abdullah would have been with me and the whole experience, all the experiences I was having, would have been heightened by their presence. But it was not to be and we all have a path to travel and sometimes it can be a long and lonely road.

With these thoughts I head for my land of magicians and pre-Islamic forts, pagan Oman, where sorcerers lie in wait for potential victims for sacrifice or turn them into the living dead. These are all stories that I had heard from my students who were utterly convinced of the truth surrounding these stories. Any student from Bahla, the centre of sorcery and the next town on my itinerary, would be pointed out to me and I would be told, "Be careful, Teacher, this man is from Bahla." Whenever I asked a student from Bahla what car he drove, the rest of the students would tell me that he did not need a car as sorcerers travel on the back of hyenas: they can fly through the sky. There definitely are hyenas in Oman, this I know from experience. One night while I was sleeping alone in the desert I was awoken by the sound of feral dogs howling and running around the periphery of where I was camping. I opened my eyes and looked down only to see a jackal about three feet away from the bottom of my blanket. Strange thing was I was not in any way afraid, it did slink off. I was more concerned about the wild dogs. When I told this story to my students they were aghast, assuring me that there was a wizard around and I could have been taken or changed into an animal or forced into being one of the living dead. I knew that the deterrent to these sorcerers was that anyone whose body contained mercury or alcohol would be immune to the powers of any wizard, therefore with my alcohol intake I felt confident that no decent self-respecting wizard would come anywhere near me. However I did not tell my students this. And from past experiences with the jinn I was more than a little wary of all things unknown. I was interested in going to Bahla to see if I could detect any of these sorcerers. I had asked the students how I would recognize a wizard. They were described to me as old men with long white beards, in which case that could be the whole of the elderly male population of Oman.

I was also very keen on seeing the pre-Islamic fort. It is thought to be about sixteen hundred years old, but very little is known about who built it and what the culture or religion was. Information lies deep in the recesses of the dark rich past of Omani history about which very little is known but research is still going on. The fort can be seen just as you enter Bahla on the brow of a hill commanding the whole plain. A veritable fortress, much, much larger than I had thought it to be, one can see the old outer walls that must have marked the perimeter of this fortressed city, as that was indeed what it must have been. Unfortunately I could not go in as it was being renovated and excavated at the same time. Very little is published about the findings. I do not know why, unless it is because that it is pre-Islamic and there may be some sensitive issue regarding what may have been found out about the Omani people and their culture before Islam. I recall the tales of Merlin in the English Dark Ages and the reign of King Arthur, Mordred, underground caves, herbal hallucinogenic, and the root of mandrake, the worship of stones and holy rocks and the ritualistic ceremonies at night under the moonlight. Human sacrifice. Could all of this have been common in pre-Islamic Oman?

Bahla is now the town that surrounds this fort. I turn right at the brow of the hill on which the fort is situated and drive into what appears to be a bustling little market town, which is exactly what it is. Apart from its sorcerers Bahla is famous for its pottery, made in the traditional way. I leave my car in the village square. I never lock it, never have since I have been here; there is no stealing from vehicles here and I have never met anyone who has had anything stolen from their car. I walk through the market, wary of any glances from old men with white beards, and find the pottery section of the market. The kilns are basic and simple and I watch as pots are cast in the way they have been for who knows how long. A lot of the pots are those water carriers which keep the water cool and clay incense burners and all sorts of pots whose function I did not know. After a couple of hours I feel I have seen Bahla: a jaunty, happy little town whose inhabitants are friendly enough. I return to my car, having escaped the wizards of Bahla, and drive to Jabrine Castle which is renowned for its scholars and is only twelve kilometres away. So now I am about to leave the home of magicians and off to visit the castle of scholars.

From the road twelve kilometres after Bahla you can see rising above an oasis of palm trees the turrets of the castle of Jibreen. You turn left and just head you stumble onto an oasis. When you arrive at Jibreen you find a castle of substantial size with a gateway and large inner courtyard. It is perhaps my favourite fort/ castle in Oman. It is certainly very beautiful and this is largely due to the recent renovations that have taken place here. It was built around 1675 in the years of the Al-Yoruba dynasty, in the heady days of the Omani Empire, by one Imam, Bilarub bin Sultan, who lived there until he died in 1692. From the castle roof one has staggering views along the Western Hajar Mountains and from the other side one can see to the horizon where lies The Empty Quarter, the Rub Alkali, where a border exists between Oman and Saudi Arabia, a very sandy border that shifts with the dunes that are moved by the desert winds.

Jibreen Castle was in fact built as a private residence for the Imam and whereas Nizwa was his political capital, Jibreen was where he would come to relax. He also established Jibreen as the greatest centre of learning in Oman. Among the many students who studied there were followers of Islamic Law, History, Arabic, Medicine and Astronomy and Astrology.

In Jibreen Castle one finds artefacts from all over the world including fine Chinese porcelain that was loaded onto the Arabian dhows in the Chinese port of Canton and off-loaded at the port of Sohar, the reputed home of Sinbad, and then brought across the mountain ranges, by camel caravans to the interior of Oman. Artefacts from Britain, Europe, Japan, India and Zanzibar also found their way to Jibreen by Arabian sail and Arab caravans.

When entering the castle you will find the old date store stained black with the resin of stored dates and many bats have made it their home. On the ground floor is a mock-up of a traditional kitchen where the falaj runs through. There is a separate prayer room for ladies. The tomb of the Imam also lies within the walls of this most intriguing of castles. All over, the light casts shadows as its rays pierce the narrow slits that were put there for defensive purposes. On the top floors one finds a Quranic schoolroom laid out as it would have been originally and nearby one of the two mosques in the castle; the other one is situated in the outer courtyard. What one must not miss at all and in my mind are the most spectacular rooms in the castle are the rooms of the Sun and the Moon. These rooms lie side by side and in one the ceiling is painted as the Moon and in the other the ceiling is painted as the Sun. In both these rooms cushions lie scattered on the floor where the weary traveller can take the weight of his feet and sit in these oh so cool rooms away from the blinding heat outside and recharge his batteries. Many a time I have done this and as often as not had a little doze. It takes a little while to find all these different features of this fort as there seem to be no end to the number of staircases within the castle wall. It is said that the Imam stabled his horse in one of the rooms in the upper half of the castle next to the Imam's Quarters. The horse was led up to its quarters by a ramp that today is a staircase.

After having some rest in the room of the Moon I leave the castle and continue my journey to the Bedu area of Dara, the capital being Ibri, leaving behind me the wonders of Dakhliyah that began in Fanja, brought me to Nizwa to the deserted village of Tanuf, up the mountain to the City of Stone, into the town of sorcerers and finally to the home of Omani scholars. I am about to enter the land that one traveller described as being a land peopled by the real Bedouin. Sounds like my kind of town.

DARA/IBRI

It is some twenty kilometres after Jibreen that we enter the region of Dara. It is true that even now this region is not very often visited by Westerners. There is not a great deal here for them – gravelly desert plains, with a few desert shrubs, some granite mountains devoid of vegetation. All in all it is quite an austere region.

This region has one of the smallest populations in Oman and most of those are descended from the Bedu and different tribes thereof who are very nomadic in their ways. Those Bedu who live in the mountains are known as "Shouwi" or mountain Bedu. They are a hardy people and slightly less friendly than the Bedu of Sharqiyah. One feels as though they have no desire for foreigners to see their way of life despite the creature comforts that the West has to offer. They are a fiercely independent people. Abdullah is from this area and I remember once when we were in a shopping mall in Muscat how fiercely he remarked on how alien he found the culture of a Western metropolis to be. He would take any opportunity to go back to his home near the desert and his camels and sleep out in the open with them. I often did this with him and wonder if he is now in his village just outside of Ibri.

So I head towards Ibri, the gravelly sand on both sides of the road with the mountains a long way in the distance, the outline of their peaks barely visible. The Western Hajar range that would eventually take me back to Batinah, the old camel route, into Sohar and then travel south back to Muscat thus completing a full circle of Northern Oman. I am left with only the southern province of Dhofar to visit which would complete my journey through the Sultanate of Oman.

The oncoming traffic has their hazard warning lights flashing on their cars. It signals either an accident ahead, or camels crossing. I slow down to see ten or more camels ambling across the road. Car horns do not impinge on their journey, they seem to look at you with contempt and then turn away and continue unruffled. Camels are marvellous creatures and the Bedu owes his very existence to them, for carrying him long distances and providing him with milk to drink and eventually meat to eat. I often wondered why Darwin never included camels in *The Origin of Species*; they have adapted themselves so perfectly to their environment that they alone would bear testament to his theory of evolution.

As I approach Ibri plantations begin to appear.

Before I arrive in Ibri, some five kilometres away, I see an old ruined village perched on a mountainside and a sign that says Sulayf. Fascinated as I am by these ruined citadels of past Oman I turn left and head for this village. It is very hot now and most people are asleep. Yet this village beckons me unto her and I take heed. I leave my car and immediately I find myself walking up a steep incline.

There is a large wooden door that marks the entrance to this city. It is hot, just after midday, and there is this ever-present stillness in the hot air that one always feels at this time of day when all creatures have taken shade from the midday sun. In some of the old Omani cities one is aware that they were in fact fortresses, designed to keep marauders out, and in Dara it was particularly important to have a city that could defend itself.

On entering I pass abandoned houses that sit on this mountain. The people here must have literally lived on top of each other. There is no space between buildings at all and it is impossible to see where one sand/mud brick dwelling finished and another began. I climbed further up, determined to reach the summit, at the top of which I could see a tower-like building. The incline becomes steeper as I stop for breath and realize why this city was built where she was. The panoramic views are incredible, 360 degrees of them and when I eventually reach the top I climb into the shaded watchtower and see that it would be impossible for anyone to attack this place without first having been seen. And so I see into the past: Oman a land of small kingdoms, chieftains, raiders, Bedu, one tribe warring with another, perhaps over some incident that happened generations ago. The Omanis would always carry arms, be fiercely loyal to their tribes, without which no individual could survive, constantly on their guard, night and day, sentries posted throughout the cites. This is Oman, a land of watchtowers on hilltops, oases, plantations, deserts, quicksand, wadis, shifting dunes, deserted villages, ruined fortressed cities all refusing to give up the secrets of their past which they so jealously guard and which I so zealously seek out.

I climb back down to my car, back into the twenty-first century, longing to know the people of the centuries gone by. It is now approaching dusk and there is a gentle breeze coming off the gravel desert plains. I drink some water, start the engines and wind down the windows and head off for the old souq of Ibri which should by now just be opening for business.

Driving into Ibri, one encounters a very large mosque with a golden dome. The rest of Ibri that I drive through is a sprawling mass of new concrete breeze block buildings, shop fronts, villas, houses. It is not particularly attractive and I am happy when I reach a small roundabout that tells me to turn right for the souq. As I drive to the souq the road turns into a dusty track and people are walking on both sides, the women in black from head to foot. The men are in traditional dishdasha and turbans, most are sporting beards and have a fierce look about them. I do feel the eyes staring, or is it just my imagination, as I drive through the now throng of people and try and find a place to park in the souq. Ibri and her people are very puritanical. It is the one region in Oman where though they have accepted tourists may visit and have built one token hotel, alcohol is severely prohibited. These are an austere and very proud and traditional conservative people.

I find a place to park and walk around in a very crowded market place; goats, sheep and cattle are tethered here and there randomly, there is a lot of bartering going on and an earthy smell persists around the souq. There is an old fort in the middle which I would dearly like to enter but somehow it seems inappropriate to do so. Fruit and vegetables are also on sale everywhere and Indian migrant workers stand around seemingly without purpose, staring unabashedly. A group of young bearded Bedu Omani men squat in the shade of one stall and bring out small pipes and pouches that contain a type of tobacco; these they fill and inhale deeply, the smoke soon drifting around the stall. Night-time has come and with the Spartan lighting I see only half faces and shadows moving around the souq. I begin to feel slightly claustrophobic. I decide to get into my car and drive away.

When I have left the souq area I find myself in the new part of town, where there seem to be fewer people around. The present Sultan of Oman has brought together very disparate regions and tribes into a consensual peace that benefits all tribes. In these days almost all villages throughout Oman are made up of several tribes, each having a leader known as a Sheikh. Yet the head of the whole town is known as the Wali and if there is a dispute between two tribes or more, for example over grazing rights, it is the Wali who will make the final judgment and it is he who represents his town or area at government level. The Wali of a town or area wields considerable power and influence.

I turn left at the mosque and drive towards the mountains which will take me to Khabourra, a village near Sohar, which is about two hundred and fifty kilometres from my base in Muscat. However it is a long drive and I am feeling weary. I think about sleeping in the desert here but somehow I want to complete my journey this very evening. I drive past Abdullah's village, which is on the way to the mountains, and take the dusty track that will lead me to the foot of the Western Hajar. The mountain trip is a hazardous one even in the day and at night many would think it was foolhardy. I arrive where the mountains begin to climb, the moon is full and if God is good then I shall arrive safely on the other side. It is only sixty kilometres of mountain road but with steep inclines, sharp turns, potholes and boulders strewn over these mountain passes. And so I am to begin the crossing and travel from the region of Dara to the region of Batinah. The Granite Mountains loom large as I begin my trek; they are bathed in moonlight and all around are the elements of nature: the trees, the rocks and stones, the nocturnal animals. The very mountains themselves tell me that this is their time; night belongs to them and so I travel in the knowledge that I too have become part of this nether world and I, along with everything else, belong to the night and the moon and the stars that guide me from above and it is they who will be the final arbiters of my fate on this journey.

The Gods guided me safely across the mountains and back into Muscat. I arrived home at about midnight and sat on the terrace with looking out onto the Indian Ocean. Never has a journey felt so vital. I feel the very essence of Oman is in my soul and sense it shall remain there for a long time. I know that my journey across Oman will not be complete until I get the opportunity to visit Dhofar, more than one thousand kilometres from Muscat. Fortunately for me, that opportunity is to arise much sooner than I could have dared hope for.

THE SUMMONING

The next day back at work I was summoned to see the colonel, Colonel Abdullah. One does not usually get summoned to see the headman unless there is something amiss. So racking my brains to try and find out what misdemeanour I had committed, I marched up the stairs to his office, which was appropriately situated at the end of the corridor. I felt like a child again, being summoned by the headmaster, for playing truant or smoking in the lavatory .I walked down the long corridor and with due respect I knocked on the door and entered. "Salaam Alakeum," I said, "Alakeum Salaam," he replied. His was a large office and he sat behind a large desk in a very comfortable large office chair. Well of course he would have all these trimming as he was the headman and due deference is paid out here to your status in the organization.

"How are you sir?"

"Fine thanks you, Rory, and you?"

"Oh fine."

"Have a seat." His face was beaming with a wonderful smile. I really was wondering why I was summoned; it did not look as though I had trespassed on anyone or anything.

"Well, Rory, how do you like your work here in Muscat?"

"Oh very much, sir." I could not quite fathom what was going on, there was something lurking there and I knew that we would reach the destination in due course. However the Arab rarely gets to the point directly, he prefers to meander with social niceties and then hit you with a request. After what has been considered a reasonable time and due protocol has been adhered to, which consists of asking you about your health, your family, your work, he will come to the point and so the Colonel did.

"Do you know Thumrait," he asked.

"I have heard of it," I replied. Of course I knew about Thumrait, I had never visited it but had read about it. Thumrait was in Dhofar, some nine hundred kilometres from Muscat, eight hundred of those virgin desert, and about ninety kilometres from Salalah. It was in the desert about thirty kilometres from the Qara Mountains that dominate the fertile plain where Salalah sits. I had read Thesiger's *Arabian Sands* and knew that it was an Omani Air force Base dating back to the 1940s. However the most fascinating aspect of Thumrait for me was that this is where it all began. This is where Wilfred Thesiger was stationed before he embarked on that seminal journey through the Empty Quarter narrated in Arabian Sands. I had dreamed of treading in his footsteps, to drink, sleep and eat in the same Officers' Mess. It was from here that he arranged all the logistics for his journey. From here he went into Salalah to arrange Bedu guides to take him so far and arrange other tribes to complete one of the most enduring travellers' tales ever undertaken. I had read and fantasized about Thesiger's trips and even wondered what Thumrait was like, the point of origin of the adventure of all adventures. Before Thesiger only two Europeans had crossed the Empty Quarter; that was Bertrand Thomas in 1930 who crossed the desert from south to north and a few months later Thomas with St. John Philby crossed it again from north to south. It was on Bertrand Thomas's first crossing that he noticed an ancient camel caravan route which was eventually to lead to the discovery of "The Lost City of Ubar", ("The Atlantis of the Desert Sands"). The Lost City of Ubar dates back to 3000 BC and was a major city on the caravan trail to the north of Arabia. It is actually situated only some eighty kilometres from Thumrait and I shall recall my trip to Ubar later in the book.

"Rory, are you with us?" I realized that I had been daydreaming when the Colonel brought me back down to earth.

"Ah yes, sir, just thinking."

"Well," he said, "there has never been an English Language training facility down there nor has there been an English Language teacher. With the new aircraft coming and the expansion of the airbase down there we need someone to train our prospective pilots in American English and generally set up an English training centre there, so that those in need of English do not have to come up to Muscat and so waste valuable manpower time."

"Yes, sir," I said, wondering what this had to do with me.

"Well," he said, "we think you are the man for the job, we would like you to do it. What do you think?" I couldn't believe my luck and on opening my mouth nothing came out. I think the Colonel thought that this was a sign that I was horrified at the prospect; on the contrary I was delighted.

"Ah yes, sir, that's fine, great I mean, when do I leave?"

"Oh, right so you are interested, well I will get the necessary paperwork completed, inform the Station Commander in Thumrait that you will be coming and he will arrange suitable accommodation and messing for you. Now as for transport down there, you can fly with the Hercules C 130."

This is a four-engine propeller aircraft that is very versatile and has been used as a troop carrier, to carry vehicles and supplies on relief missions. On the C 130 one sits in columns that stretch from one end of the aircraft to another and opposite you is another column of passengers so that you are touching knees with your neighbour. Well the first time I flew into the desert on the C130 I felt as though I were in a Second World War movie and that any moment now the bay doors would open and I would be dropped out and parachuted into occupied France. There are no windows for the passengers to look out so I managed to maintain this fantasy for the duration of the trip, about two hours.

"Well, sir I have my car which I will need in Salalah and Thumrait, can the C130 take that down?"

"No I am afraid not, you could get it transported down or drive down."

"Drive I think, sir."

"Well Rory, Alright, Inshallah, we will let you know when all is ready so you can pack up and go to Thumrait, good luck."

"Thank you, sir," I replied and left the office in a state of elation. My wildest dreams had come true and I was about to complete the final chapter in my voyage around Oman. The area I was to visit was the biblical place of the Tomb of the Prophet Job, The lost City of Ubar, and the land of the Queen of Sheba, the Stone Age world of the Al-Shara tribe, the green lush Qara Mountains and the source of wealth even greater than gold, frankincense. I could hardly contain myself.

THE ROAD TO THUMRAIT

I began to pack my things and get ready to spend some time in Dhofar. I was slightly concerned about the journey and how I was going to get there yet I thought things would eventually sort themselves out. I packed six trunks full of gear and drove them all to the military cargo area at the airport, where they would be transported down to Thumrait by the Hercules C 130 and be ready for me to collect on arrival. I had decided that I would drive down and not have my car sent by transport lorry. I also decided that I could not face eighteen hours driving in a military convoy. The decision I had made was that I would drive myself to Thumrait, risk the perils of a breakdown, soaring temperatures of over 50 degrees Celsius, shifting sand dunes that sometimes blocked the road, raging dust devils and wandering camels and that I would…Inshallah…arrive safely in Thumrait.

Early one Thursday morning at 4.30a.m. I left my apartment in Muscat and began my journey to Thumrait. It was still dark and the stars were visible and a half moon hung suspended in the sky. I drove out of Muscat on completely empty roads, arrived at the roundabout that marks the beginning of Muscat, Birkat Al Sahwa, and headed for Nizwa where I would pick up the desert road to Thumrait, eighty kilometres from Salalah. As I drove past the Gun souq of Fanja and Birkat Al Mawz, the entrance to Jebel Akdhar, the Green Mountain, the dawn was beginning to break over the mountains of the Western Hajar. This was my favourite time of day in Oman and in all other desert countries that I have ever visited. The air smells fresh and almost sweet. There is always a slight breeze and you are drawn to stop the vehicle that you are driving and stand outside and just enjoy that precious half hour when the new day is dawning and everything feels like a new beginning in your life... That day was no exception and as I stood outside the car, in the shadow of the second highest mountain in Oman, my thoughts were cast back to all those places that I had been and all those people I had met in Oman, and that now I was indeed on the last phase of my voyage and what it had to bring to me I had no idea, yet if it brought me just half the wealth of experiences I had had so far I would be more than happy.

So I reached the end of the mountain road and the roundabout at which before I had turned right and driven to Nizwa and then onto Tanuf, Bahla, Ibri and across the mountains back to Muscat. This time I turned left and headed for Salalah, nine hundred kilometres, eight hundred kilometres of which were desert. So with the sun on my right and a smile on my face I drove through the gears and headed out to drive through the desert sands of Oman as featured in *Arabian Sands*.

Five hundred miles, eight hundred kilometres of virgin desert to drive before I reach my place of work. I have heard of commuting but this is ridiculous. I feel the heat of the desert building up in the car and turn the air conditioning up to its maximum. It is a desolate area of Oman; there are few vehicles on the road, as yet no villages. The next petrol stop is two hundred kilometres at a desert town called Al-Hayma. This town has sprung up to service vehicles travelling to and from Salalah as this road is the one and only road to Salalah. It is also a market town where the local Bedu can come and sell livestock, buy supplies and then return into the desert. Until then I drive along a deserted desert highway. I keep looking to my right where the Empty Quarter lies and try to imagine the hardship endured by Thesiger. It is only 10a.m. but it is already 48 Celsius outside. I, in the comfort of an air cooled car, can only wonder how he managed, in these temperatures, to put up with what he did. This I will never know how and if the truth be told I do not want to find out how. I have an adventurous spirit but only up to a point.

This is the area where Oman's oil fields are to be found. Oman has oil and gas but not in as great abundance as Saudi Arabia and the money here has been used wisely on infrastructure: roads, schools, education, hospitals and housing, all of which were absent before the 1970s. Oman has come a long way under the rule of the present Sultan.

On my left is the desert and coastal region of Al Wusta, a land full of untamed Bedu, the most sparsely and arguably most beautiful area of Oman, with its wildlife and deserted shores that feature wind- and sand-eroded rocks and cliffs making it look like a natural park full of abstract rock sculptures. Many shipwrecks have been left where they sank on this coast and have themselves attracted a wealth of marine life. It is in the Al Wusta region that we find the Jiddat which is an enormous nature reserve protected by the Harasis Bedu tribesmen who act as park rangers. It is here that the Arabian oryx has been introduced again after it became extinct in 1974 through irresponsible hunting. Now there are said to be over three hundred wild oryx in this area, protected by the Harasis. They are a splendid sight, from the antelope family, but they are white which reflects the sunlight and also acts as camouflage in the brilliant sun. They can do without water for a long spell; they get their water from grazing on the desert plants and have adapted their digestive systems to absorb almost all of the water content of any plant they eat. What a wonderfully diverse country Oman is and with such a small population one finds here the harmony of nature and man living together, co-existing with and respecting one another.

I stop at Al Hayma to fill my nearly depleted petrol tank. By now it is over 50 degrees Celsius. Al Hayma is a busy little desert town and the people are milling around, obviously with great purpose. There are some trucks in the petrol station full of calves making their way up north to be sold in the markets of Nizwa, Rustaq or Ibri. Other small pickups carry goats that they are bringing to the market here to sell and the money they receive from this they will spend on food provisions, rice, flour etc. Everyone is going somewhere or doing something. Few people actually live here, apart from the Indian ex-pats who work in the various shops that sell the provisions.

I fill up my tank, buy some bottles of water and head out of Hayma. Still to my right the forbidding Empty Quarter dominates the landscape. It is said that when God divided the world into the sea and land, he left this as the Empty Quarter, The Rub Alkali. It is also rumoured that here lies, somewhere buried beneath the dunes, the fabulous ancient city of Ubar, and called by T. E. Lawrence "The Atlantis of the sands". Ubar was said to have been created as an imitation of paradise. It was said to be built by King Shaddad, son of King Ad, grandson of Noah. So indeed this area does have biblical ties. It was a major city on the frankincense route to the north of Arabia and beyond. It was a veritable oasis and had magnificent gardens and its people led a heady and decadent life, such was the wealth that was there and it was largely created by the Frankincense trade. The site dates back to 3000 BC and as I drive along the Empty Quarter I begin to get excited as the site of this lost city lies only eighty kilometres this side of my destination in a village now known as Shisur. The site was said to have disappeared beneath the sands after a violent earthquake. Indeed it was mentioned in the Koran as a godless city that brought upon itself the wrath of Allah. This ancient town has featured for centuries in the oral storytelling tradition of the Bedu. However the Bedu believed that it was the decadence and hedonism of these people of Ubar that incurred the wrath of God who then destroyed the city when the people refused to change their ways and the sands opened up and swallowed them all.

So was this a city of mere legend or was it based on fact? As I said Bertrand Thomas first noticed the ancient caravan trail in his epic crossing of the Empty Quarter. After this many expeditions were launched to find the Lost City of Ubar yet they all failed and people began to doubt the existence of such a place. However the NASA scientists, in the 1990s, agreed to alter the space shuttle's flight plan and steered it around to the Empty Quarter. They beamed a powerful radar signal to Earth and revealed images of what indeed could be a city under the sands dating back to 3000 BC which was when Ubar was said to have been built. After this revelation an expedition led by Sir Ranulph Fiennes went in search of Ubar. After several aborted digs they came upon the fairly new town of Al Shisur. After exchanging pleasantries with the local Sheikhs who themselves told stories about a lost civilisation that dealt with the frankincense trade, the Sheikhs told them there were some ruins at the back of the village that were about five hundred years old. When the archaeologists accompanying Fiennes started their dig they found the foundations a lot deeper than expected and then found very ancient artefacts. In fact the ruins were not five hundred years old but five thousand years old and coincided exactly with the time span that the city of Ubar occupied. So the ancient city of Ubar had at last been uncovered and the Empty Quarter had given up one of its many secrets.

As I drive through the now scorching desert I see a sign for Shisur to the right. As I take this turn and drive along, my mind imagines a time five thousand years ago when caravans of three thousand camels carrying frankincense and myrrh would be walking towards the hedonistic town of Ubar and wished that I had been around for a bit of that decadence myself. As I enter Shisur I find it very much like any other village and the excavations themselves appear to be small. There is a museum here with a limited number of artefacts so some people may be disappointed. However it takes only a little imagination as you gaze on those dunes and the vast empty spaces to transport yourself in time and space and be an observer of a magnificent spectacle such as a camel caravan and all its exotic attendants entering a city that was created in the image of paradise.

I leave Shisur and find my way back to the desert highway which will take me to Thumrait. There are only eighty kilometres left to drive and it is getting towards dusk. I am still excited about living in the same place as Thesiger did all those years ago. Shortly after I see the beginnings of an airbase and some single storey sand-coloured buildings. Thumrait, turn right, three kilometres, the road sign says and so I do. I pass through the security gate into the former home of perhaps the greatest explorer and adventurer of the twentieth century. I have finished one memorable journey and shall use Thumrait as a base for further explorations, this time into the land of Dhofar.

IN SEARCH OF THE QUEEN OF SHEBA

We have talked so much about the land of the Queen of Sheba, the cargoes of precious stones, vast quantities of gold, spices and frankincense transported throughout the ancient world by her kingdom, but how much do we really know about her and the land of her people?

Who exactly was the Queen of Sheba? Most people have heard tales about her. Hollywood films have been made of her. She is probably one of the most famous and enduring of all women throughout history. Yet how much do we actually know about her and how much of that is based on archaeological fact? Was she the stuff of mere myth and legend or did she exist in history? Well the answer to the first question is that there is no hard archaeological evidence to support her existence, no inscriptions on temples, no trace of her in any of the archaeological digs. Neither is there any evidence to support the fact that King Solomon existed. Was she just a myth or did she exist in reality or does she fall somewhere between the two? Do myths and legends have their roots in facts? Well the answer to that is usually yes.

No hard scientific evidence exists to support the fact that she was a real person; however, she is featured as a real historical figure in the writings of the Bible, the Koran, the Ethiopian Book of Kings, and later Jewish chronicles and even in the New Testament. Probably the most mentioned woman in all of the world's monotheistic religions. Where did she actually come from? She is said to come from the land of Saba, but where exactly was the land of Saba. Early scholars believed that the land of Saba was in Ethiopia. This is because in the Ethiopian Book of Kings, the Queen of Sheba, the first of the Ethiopian imperial family, who is named Makeda, was said to have visited Solomon in the tenth century BC, bringing with her frankincense, spices, precious stones and many other gifts including four thousand kilograms of gold. According to Ethiopian history she was born in 1020 BC and educated in Ethiopia. Her mother was Queen Ismenie and her father was one Za Sebado.

One story describes that as a child she was bitten by a hyena that left one of her legs permanently scarred and in the Koran she is described as having one leg like that of a goat or ass. It is said that when she first went to Solomon's palace the floor was made of crystal glass and was mirrored. She, looking on this mirrored floor, thought it was a lake. As she hitched up her dress to avoid it getting wet, it was then that her bad leg was reflected in the floor, leading the courtiers to rumour that she had one leg the same as an animal. She was said to have worshipped the Sun and Moon and in fact the religion of Saba was pantheistic. Why did she want to visit Solomon? Well according to all the scriptures she had heard of the great wisdom of this man and as a queen she valued wisdom beyond all earthly treasures.

"I desire wisdom and my heart seeketh to find understanding. I am smitten with the love of wisdom…for wisdom is far better than treasure of gold or silver…it is sweeter than honey…it is a source of joy for the heart…it makes the ears to hear and the heart to understand…and as for a kingdom, it cannot stand without wisdom, and riches cannot be preserved without wisdom." (*The Ethiopian Book of Kings*.)

So, according to Ethiopian history, the Queen of Sheba, Makeda, visited Solomon and they fell in love. On her return to Ethiopia she was said to have brought two special gifts. One was a gold ring given to her by Solomon and the second, more precious gift, was the baby in her stomach: Solomon's child. She gave birth and named him Menelik and he became the first ruler of the first tribe of the Lion of Judah and it was from him that all Ethiopian rulers descended, including the last Solomonic monarch in 1974, Haile Selassie. Modern day Rastafarians would see themselves as descendants of Menelik and his mother. It is said that when Menelik came of age he went to see his father Solomon and at first his father did not believe who he was; and then Menelik produced the ring that Solomon had given to Menelik's mother. Solomon then rejoiced and invited Menelik to govern with him side by side, but Menelik said he wanted to return home to his mother and eventually rule his own kingdom. Solomon was sad but let his son go. However he is said to have given him one of the great treasures from his temple: the Ark of the Covenant.

This, according to Ethiopian history, was brought back to Ethiopia and to this day all Ethiopians believe it is housed in the church of St. Mary of Zion in the ancient Ethiopian city of Axum. It is of no surprise then that modern scholars say that there was a link between Judea and an ancient African queen that led to the emergence of Judaism in Ethiopia.

Archaeological digs recently have found a temple in the most ancient of Ethiopian cities which date back to 900 BC yet that is too late for the Queen of Sheba. However, writings on this temple were the same as those found in Yemen that date back to 1100 BC which would coincide with the reign of the Queen of Sheba. It is now practically certain that the ancient land of Saba is situated in present day Yemen and that this civilisation was trading with the Egyptians as far back as 2000 BC and that the trade of frankincense, that was prized above all others, that burnt in the ancient temples of Egypt, did indeed come from the land of Saba, which included also the area in Oman known as Dhofar, where most of the frankincense is harvested. So Dhofar was part of the ancient kingdom of Saba and the frankincense trail went by land northwards past the Lost City of Ubar to areas such as Damascus, Babylon etc. and seawards up the Red Sea to ancient Egypt. It is also quite certain that the Kingdom of Saba had strong trading links with Ethiopia where she traded her wares for African goods such as ivory. Indeed at the shortest point there is only fifteen miles of sea separating Yemen from Ethiopia on the horn of Africa. It may be that at one time the kingdom of Saba included Ethiopia and that

Menelik, son of Solomon and Sheba, ruled Ethiopia while his mother sat on the throne in Yemen. In short it is almost certain that a Sabaean empire existed, based in Yemen, but including much of the horn of Africa and of course Dhofar.

THE TRIBESPEOPLE OF THE MOUNTAINS
OF AL-QARA

The indigenous people of Dhofar are racially and linguistically different from those of northern Oman.

Dhofar is separated from Muscat by some eleven hundred kilometres. It is the land of a classical age, of frankincense, caravans of up to a thousand camels carrying their exotic cargoes to the destinations of the empires of Assyria, Egypt, Phoenicia and many more that were predominant in the ancient world more than five thousand years ago. This is the only area in Oman where frankincense trees grew and so this was the starting point of the distribution throughout the classical world and is associated with so many myths, legends and history all intertwined that it is impossible to distinguish myth from reality, if there is a difference at all.

The indigenous peoples of Dhofar are largely a pastoral people and tend herds of camels, cattle, sheep and goats. There, mountains are more like hills than mountains and indeed in the monsoon they are wrapped in thick clouds and fog and during this time the mountains turn to a lush green, meadows abound, and after the fog has cleared you can travel through the country roads of the mountains of Dhofar, watch the cattle graze in the green fields and feel yourself to be in the countryside in Ireland, certainly not Arabia. Many a time I had to stop my car to allow cattle to cross from one field to another and the earthy smell brought me back to my childhood and those glorious holidays I passed in Ireland with my parents and their families. The only difference here was that the cattle herder wore a sarong, was bare-chested and on his shoulder a rifle was slung, and strapped over his chest from one side to another was a bandolier. His hair was quite long and physically he was lean and wiry. Indeed the resilience and strength of these mountain people manifested itself to me when one day I stopped to let cattle cross and saw that the cattle herder had only one leg and used a crutch to support himself. How he managed the terrain and his whole work with just one leg is difficult to comprehend.

The villages, too, in Dhofar are built in a completely different way and they tend to be more like hamlets than villages. The typical house will look something like a European farmhouse with many outbuildings in which to house their livestock. On the coast of Salalah and in Salalah it is different, far more like Muscat, but the people here are generally Arab and mixed race. The people who live in the mountains are referred to as Jabali; Jebel in Arabic means mountain, so Jabali means mountain people. However their real tribal name is the people of the Al-Shahra tribe and they speak a language known as Al-Shari. This is a very ancient language and it is oral, there is no written form. Only about ten thousand people still speak this language and if it is not recorded then it will soon be extinct. Social anthropologists have said that these people have been here for thousands of years and pre-date the arrival of the Arab from Yemen by thousands of years. Indeed one Jabali friend took me to his village after I had expressed an interest in cave painting, and in the mountains took me to caves where I found amazing drawings; they were not coloured but black and white and showed men and animals. I was dumbfounded and never revealed the location of these paintings, and till this day I have not. This was a lovely little hamlet and to destroy its rhythm of life by turning it into a tourist circus destination was something I was not prepared to do and am still not. Yet I would dearly like to date these paintings and know more about the culture that drew them. Intuitively I feel that it was the very people who live in the mountains now and speak the ancient tongue of Al-Shari.

During the Monsoon the tribes from the mountains bring their livestock down to the plains of Salalah as the mountains become slippery and treacherous for their livestock and in the markets of Salalah you can find these mountain tribesmen. While the mountain tribes are of a different racial and linguistic nature, in the coastal towns of Salalah, Mirbat and Taqa dwell descendants from other nations bearing testimony to the fact that as in any other trading/seafaring nation, the coast will be one big melting pot of nationalities and races and the coastal region of Dhofar is no exception.

The hills of Dhofar are beautiful and lush, in particular the Qara Mountains. To the south-west the mountains become desert-like and it is here, (where the ancient frankincense trees grow, the resin of which was the source of fabulous wealth for this area), which was now thought to be part of the Kingdom of Saba, over which the Queen of Sheba ruled and which is now known as the Yemen. The green parts of the mountains of Qara are said by some to be the place the Bible was written and indeed when travelling around this area the topography is very much like that described in the Old Testament. In one of the mountains the tomb of the prophet Job is to be found. He is also recognized by the followers of Islam as a prophet. So Dhofar is an ancient biblical land, a land where secrets and wonders are buried beneath the surface and where you feel that you are travelling in a special, spiritual realm. Eagles dominate the skies, soaring by in majestic grace on the thermals high above the mountains of Dhofar.

THE TRIBESPEOPLE OF THE MOUNTAINS OF AL-QARA. PART TWO

Being in a civilian officer in the Sultan's Armed Forces we would usually have much longer public holidays than those in the public centre. I made my mind up to take advantage of this and continue my journeys of discovery in the Dhofar area. I therefore left the base at Thumrait early one morning at six o'clock and drove through the forty kilometres that separated the desert from the Mountains of Qara. This area of desert is austere and peopled by Bedu. Camels are in abundance here and one has to drive carefully through this winding desert road to avoid colliding with a camel crossing the road, which would mean certain death for both camel and driver.

At the end of the desert road and the beginning of the mountains, there is an army checkpoint. Here one is stopped by army personnel and one's papers are checked. The drive from here down into Salalah is very steep and the landscape changes dramatically, livestock grazing in fields on either side of the road. No longer are you in the land of the Bedu and its accompanying desertscape, but rather a fertile area of farmers and small villages where people sell and buy livestock and agricultural produce in small market areas. It was in one such village that I used to buy fertilizer for my garden in the desert. I would drive off the main road into the village and just beyond up a muddy track where I would encounter a corrugated iron shack from where I would buy sacks of dry fertilizer. Here cattle would pass me by, driven by their Jabali herdsmen, into pastures where they would graze and then move on in time-honoured fashion to the next field and eventually complete a circuit, at the end of which they would arrive back home to their point of origin and lie down for another night or be penned up in the outhouses that were built onto the main house of the Jabali residence.

Driving down the mountains one sees many villages nestled therein and also an abundance of caves which were the residences and probably now give sanctuary on stormy nights when the weather forbids a return to home and the shepherd and his flock can take shelter from the storm. I stopped my car half way down the descent into Salalah and gazed down into the valleys. The green on the top of the mountains was sparse but deep down one saw masses of green foliage that resembled forests and they were green all year around. The distance, between the top of these mountains and the valley floor where the forests bloomed, was immense and I know of no one who has actually been to explore this area. Leopards were said to have flourished here and recently there have been sightings. Hyenas are in abundance here, but being nocturnal one will not see them in the day, but at night when they venture out to hunt they will cross this mountain road and many have been seen lying on the side of the road after having been hit by cars during the night. It is an incredible place and largely unexplored.

I drove without stopping for some forty kilometres and eventually arrived at one of my destinations. This was a place known as Khor Rori; khor in Arabic means creek. From the top of the descent to the coast one could see this creek coming in from the sea and meandering its way inland some ten kilometres. At this point was a ruined citadel. This was my destination. It was believed that this was at one time a palace belonging to the Queen of Sheba and teams of Italian archaeologists have been excavating this site for a least a decade. I drove towards this ancient city along a rough track and entered through a hole in the fence. I walked around these ruins and excavations were obviously taking place where foundations had been dug away and walls were revealed. I then realized that I was walking on what once was the top of the citadel; I looked seawards and had a spectacular view. It was obvious that this had once been a major trading port with ships from the classical age making their way up the creek, unloading their cargoes of whatever they were trading and then reloading, probably with frankincense, sailing back down the creek and onto the open seas and back to their point of origin. Debate still rages about what particular era this citadel belongs to, but its position and size bears testament to the fact that in its time it played a great part in the seagoing trade in an age now lost in the mists of time.

There are many archaeological sites to be explored in Dhofar and I was determined to visit as many of these as I possibly could; however I was about two hours from Thumrait and driving through the mountains and the desert at night is something to be avoided at all costs. I therefore decided to return to my home in Thumrait. I travelled up the mountains, past the army post, and into the desert. The road was completely empty and dusk was approaching as the desert sun lowered in the sky. I was driving along, happy and content in that I had had a glimpse into the pastoral world of the Jabali and the ancient seafaring trade that the citadel of Khor Rori hosted.

THE SNAKE

Today Salalah is by and large a modern urban sprawl, apart from the Old souq where you can still walk around the old frankincense market. This is the first place many visitors from all over the world will come. Many Omani women sit cross-legged on the ground in the narrow passageways of the souq with various bags of frankincense of different quality and different prices. There are usually brightly coloured clay frankincense burners and charcoal on sale too in order to fire the frankincense. One of the most fascinating aspects of Salalah is that all around it and outside are archaeological excavations.

On one occasion just after Eid I decided to approach Salalah from another direction east along the coast. This coastal road takes you past rich vegetation, banana trees, coconut trees, and an abundance of other fruits; the sides of the road are a riot of green foliage. At every fifty metres you will find a stall selling coconuts and bananas etc. One has the sensation that one is driving in Africa not Arabia. I stopped at one of these stalls, and an Indian manning the stall, chose a green coconut, and with a machete, hacked away at this fruit, made a small hole in the top, inserted a straw and gave it to me to drink.

It was like nectar; I paid the equivalent of fifty pence, got in my car and drove away.

My journey along the coast took me past a large archaeological excavation site that was fenced off. However there was a gate and a notice board outside. Thinking that this notice board would perhaps give me some information as to the site being excavated I drove my car to the gate and got out to read the notice. The notice gave no information whatsoever regarding the site that was being dug. Rather it was a quotation from the Koran, in both English and Arabic. I shall try to paraphrase its content: "Every creature, be it animal, bird or insect, are all part of God's creation and as such deserve respect from Man, who is God's first creation." I was impressed by the sentiment expressed and drew parallels with other world religions.

I got back into the car and started to drive into the centre of Salalah. Feeling in need of some rest and refreshment I went into a hotel and inquired as to whether there was a coffee shop open. The receptionist led me outside to a great expanse of freshly cut green lawn that backed onto the Indian Ocean where waves of a brilliant blue were crashing onto the shore. Adjacent to the path was a small pile of boulders and as we were approaching I saw the unmistakable shape of a snake slithering into and disappearing down a black hole in this pile of boulders. On my return from the beachside café and arriving at the same pile of boulders I saw the head of the same snake peering around and generally surveying the area. I noticed that the snake had the markings of an Arabian cobra: a highly venomous snake, potentially fatal. The voice of my education said to me "Kill it" so I bent down to pick up a rock and raised my arm to hurl this rock at the snake. Just then my thoughts were drawn back to the notice outside the archaeological site and I realized that this snake was in its home perhaps protecting its young, as any mother would. What right did I have to take this life? I thought again about the sentiments implicit in that quote from the Koran and that if all animals, birds and insects are also part of God's creation, did not God also impart to his animals the same instincts as he passed onto his supreme creation, Man. If so then this snake was acting out of the instinct to protect her young and her home, which perhaps are the two most fundamental instincts that belong to Man, the need for a home and the need to protect and provide for his family. With these thoughts I walked carefully around the snake and back into my car and drove into Salalah where I had some work to do at a bank. Having entered the bank I engaged in conversation with a bank clerk and asked him if he had enjoyed his Eid. "Oh yes," he replied. I then told him I had just seen an Arabian cobra. "Where?" he enquired.

"In the hotel down the road. Perhaps you visited the same one with your family in Eid and the snake was also there at that time."

"Oh no," he replied. "When we are free we spend all our time at home with our family. Life is nothing without a home and a family. A man can own ten thousand camels but without a home, family or love he is a very poor man. Every man needs a home and a family." He continued, "It is not important whether this home is a palace or a hut made from bamboo." I was moved by the simplicity, candour and the priorities of life that were reflected in the sentiment of this casual conversation. Yes, I thought to myself, every creature in God's universe needs a home and it is of no importance whether this home is a grand palace, a small bamboo hut or even a pile of boulders.

THE PROPHET

As these were now holidays, I decided to continue my exploration of Dhofar. The following day I was destined to visit the tomb of Job and this is my story of that journey.

High on a mountain top in an isolated region north of Salalah lies the tomb of Job, a prophet in Judaism, Christianity and Islam. The tomb itself is housed in a small building with a distinctive dome next to a mosque. These two are perched on the edge of the mountainside with breathtaking views down into lush green valleys which lie beneath this mountain range.

My journey is to take me to this tomb, a journey which will takes three hours by car but which also take me on a journey through a time long gone and a mystical trip through three of the great monotheistic religions.

On climbing the mountain road to my destination I take a turning to the right which brings me onto a small twisting lane that leads to the foothills of the Mountains of Qara, at the bottom of which flows a natural spring. Coming to the end of the road I am faced with lush green fields on which graze goats, camels and cattle. I get out of my car to breathe in the invigorating air and take some photographs. My attention is drawn to a herd of goats behind which follows an elderly goat herder, dressed in a sarong, tee shirt and a turban and he is carrying an old British Lee Enfield rifle. I greet him in Arabic whereupon we engage in a conversation.

"Where are you from?" he asks

"From Ireland," I reply.

"Oh the same as England."

"Not exactly," I say.

"Maybe it is to the north," he continues.

"Yes, maybe," I respond.

"Where are you going?" he continues,

"To see the tomb of the prophet Job."

"You are a Muslim," he replies.

"No I am a Christian but Job is also a prophet in our religion."

"Ah, yes, the Bible, I know the book the Bible, it is a good book, and we all have the same God." I am struck by the ease and flow of his conversation and his serenity and the sense of his peace and harmony that he finds in his surroundings and his work. His desire to converse on things that are spiritually significant, but more than that his obvious inability to divorce his spiritual side from his working life: they are integrated, one, indivisible. There can be no division between them, for did not God create everything: Himself, the land, his goats and the pastures from which they feed, so how can there be any division? Not at any time am I intimidated by his rifle, in fact as our conversation continues it disappears into my subconscious and our discourse flows as smoothly as the waters from the mountain streams. "What do you do?" he asks.

"I work with the air force," I reply. His face breaks into a grin.

"I am a mere goat herder," he replies and then brings down his rifle and stands to mock attention and gives me a salute with a great smile. We both laugh together having participated in a moment in time of shared communion. We bid each other farewell, wishing upon one another the blessings of God, and he follows his herd onto fresh pastures and I myself continue onto my own fresh pastures.

I drive my car back up the lane to the junction and turn right. The road meanders steeply high into the mountains. There is no traffic at all; strangely enough I do not expect any for I feel that for me this is to be a solitary pilgrimage at the end of which I am to learn something of great value that will sustain and nurture me for the rest of my life.

The appointed time arrives when I come to the tomb of the prophet Job. I pull into the car park where I find myself to be the lone visitor. There are no other pilgrims; I feel that there were never meant to be.

I get out of my car and feel the stillness and quiet surround me. It is midday, there is no breeze, and I feel the heat of the sun burning my face. To my left I can smell the pungent, heady odour of burning frankincense. On turning to my left I see in the distance a cloud of smoke suspended just above the line of lush trees visible beneath the clear, brilliant blue skies that extend from the African Continent. I know intuitively that this is where the tomb of Job lies. I walk along a path strewn with magnificent bougainvillea in full bloom with blossoms of pink, white and orange. I smell the sweet nectar of the jasmine tree and other exotic perfumes from trees, plants and shrubs that border this twisting pathway, whose rock has been smoothed by the passing of time and by the armies of pilgrims who walked this path before me – kings, queens, and other pilgrims from the classical age that is shrouded in the mists of legends from a time long lost. This shrine, visited by so many over such great periods of time, is also my destination and I am fated to leave my footprints along with the now ghosts who have trodden this path since the dawn of time. For this place is a mystic site and always has been.

As I turn the final bend on the pathway I am confronted by a white edifice, almost square, the size of a normal house, with a green dome covering the whole roof area. Inside the edifice is the tomb of Job. There are signs outside, in both English and Arabic, asking men to remove their shoes before entering. This I do and then enter the shrine. It is a large room painted white, in the middle of which is the tomb or sarcophagus. No stone or granite is visible for the entire tomb is covered in a green material on which prayers in Arabic are woven into the fabric. There is great serenity to be found here and a profound sense of being somewhere special. The frankincense is strong and sweet, inducing you into a trance-like state through which you are transcended into another realm, where your primeval senses take over your superficial conscious self of the twenty-first century.

On leaving the shrine the custodian takes me into the courtyard. This courtyard is an area of scrubland that contains three walls that look as old as time itself; indeed I am to discover that is exactly what they are. The custodian tells me that one of these walls was built to face Jerusalem and that it is from this wall that Job knelt and prayed in the direction of that ancient mystic city. From here I am taken to a small area off the pathway where what looks like a metal trapdoor lies in the ground. The custodian lifts the trapdoor and as my eyes get accustomed to the dark I can make out a footprint in the rock. I look at the custodian inquisitively and he smiles knowingly at me. "Yes" he says, "this is the footprint of the prophet Job." For me it is like the Holy Grail. It is only then that it becomes clear to me why I have made this journey. I feel as though the custodian himself knew beforehand of my arrival. I now see him in a different light: he appears ethereal, not of this world. His enigmatic smile continues and there is a shimmering quality to his whole physical being. "Put your fingers around the outline of the footprint, feel it, rest your palm on the flat of the foot and its heel." I gaze at him, startled; for I feel to do something like this would be tantamount to sacrilege, desecration. The ethereal messenger reads my thoughts and says, "You must do this thing; it is why you have come to this place."

I lower my hand into this holy place, rest my fingers in the place where the prints of the toes were and lay the palm of my hand flat along the length of the foot. I do this carefully, slowly and with a sense of ceremony that embraces my whole being. I feel a sudden surge well up inside me and a strange sensation overcomes me that this footprint and my inner self are forever connected. It is at this exact moment that I realize why I have come and what is to be revealed. It is connected to footprints yet in a figurative way. It is about the life we lead but more importantly the legacy we leave behind after we have departed from this life. Everything we do has a consequence and leaves behind it an effect, whether great or small, and this will leave a residue, a footprint, and this footprint will affect all those around us while we live and those who follow us when we "shed this mortal coil".

We leave behind our footprints and unlike those left in the sand, these footprints cannot be washed away by the winds of time. Like the footprint of Job, they are forever with us. Those we have loved and lost, in our souls we carry their footprints. They have not gone from us, how can they when we carry their mark inside our very beings. Like mountain streams they have run their course and have entered the Great Mother Ocean of the Universe. Yet like the dried-up river beds they have left their mark for all to see, some more universally evident than others, like Moses, Jesus, Mohammed etc., yet still their mark remains within us. Our purpose in life is to leave good, unselfish and meaningful footprints in the souls of others, for them to follow, to comfort them when we depart and when our river has also run its course and entered the Great Mother Ocean of the Universe.

I remove my hand from the footprint of Job; I look around for the custodian but I know he will not be there; his task has been completed. I stand up and begin to walk away from the tomb, yet I know in my heart and soul I shall never be able to really walk away for my soul will always bear the mark of Job.

THE FINAL JOURNEY

Fatima telephoned the day after I had visited the tomb of the prophet Job. She told me Juma had died, in a car accident. Under Muslim law the body had to be buried within twenty-four hours of death. Muslims do not believe in cremation as their creed tells them that on Judgment Day the bodies shall rise whole from the grave and they will stand before God to be judged and to be deemed worthy of paradise or not. If they are cremated then their bodies cannot rise as they will be ashes. She asked me if I would come and see her. I told her I would come the following day and so I was to start what was to be my final journey in Oman.

When I heard the news my lust for adventure had been taken away from me. There were still so many sights to visit in Dhofar but my appetite was lost. I was to go and pay my condolences to Juma's family and as I set off from Thumrait I felt an overwhelming sadness. I left at dawn and had a very long and melancholy drive ahead of me. A great darkness of spirit immersed my whole being. As the desertscape passed me by so too did memories: the smiling faces of Juma and Abdullah; the old forts that we had visited; the ancient ruins of cities lost in the fog of time; the deserts we had slept out in; the mountains that we had crossed; all the sights that we had seen;

the jokes that we had shared; the lives we had shared. All of these thoughts raced through my mind as I drove along the empty desert roads with the midday sun causing shimmering mirror-like reflections off the tarmac road. I thought of the great sorrow that his family must be enduring and it burnt my very soul. For the value of a thing is never really known until it is lost to you. I drove all day, stopping only to refill the car with petrol.

After twelve hours of continuous driving I reached the outskirts of Juma's village. I pulled the car off the road into the desert and drove for a kilometre or two until I was surrounded and encircled by tall sand dunes and completely alone. I turned off the engine and walked outside. There was a great stillness, a roaring, deafening silence as I walked through the desert. I sat for a while in the hot sand and drifted off into a deep sleep. I felt a oneness with the desert as though I too belonged here. Not even in England have I felt as though I belonged there truly; my heart and soul have never really identified with the place where I was born. Is this the difference between Western man and Bedu? Has Western man lost his sense of identity with the society into which he was born? Does it have no meaning for him? Is he forever to be flotsam floating on the ocean of humanity with no particular direction? I awoke from my slumber with my cheeks dampened from tears that had fallen because of my grief and also my joy. That moment was my damascene epiphany, for it dawned on me that I had grown since I had come to Oman; spiritually I was much more aware of my condition and the condition of man. I knew that the West had it wrong: their appetites for material goods, longevity of life, a fat bank balance, an expensive car, the sacred cows of Western life, all these to be gained by an individual at any cost to anyone and anything. I knew then that this was not what life was about. I felt that I was now ready to visit Fatima. I drove into the village and to Juma's house. It was full of people mourning the loss of their friend, brother, father, cousin, husband etc. I duly paid my respects to Fatima and caught sight of Miriam. She was confused and upset by the obvious sadness that she felt from the people present, yet she was not aware that she had lost her father. The chain that hung around her neck with the miniature Koran in locket form passed through her fingers nervously. Her baby brother lay in his mother's arms, his face turned into her breast to seek comfort and shelter from the great confusion of sorrow that he was subjected to.

I desperately wanted to see the last resting place of Juma and one of his cousins told me he would take me. We drove along the dusty desert tracks for about five kilometres until we came to a small clearing. In the middle of this clearing there was a square, half the size of a football field, marked out in rough stone. Juma's cousin guided me through this Arabian cemetery to a freshly dug grave out of which protruded a single stone that marked the place where Juma lay. I stood and looked at this spot for five minutes or so. Really I have no idea for how long; with one final look I turned away and headed towards the car where Juma's cousin sat. I thought of all the times we had spent together and the best of those had been in this desert at night talking under the night skies and finally sleeping, awaking to those glorious desert sunrises. I did not feel any great yearning to retrace my footprints in the desert sand; there was no need, for I knew that part of me will forever remain in these desert sands, under the stone that marks the grave…And as we drive away from the necropolis in the desert, the sun is setting and with it the wind is blowing, covering the tombstones in a fine film of sand, and it is at that point I realize that one journey has finished and another is just about to begin.

THE END